MISTAKEN IDENTITY

MISTAKEN IDENTITY

Two Families,
One Survivor,
Unwavering Hope

Don & Susie Van Ryn and
Newell, Colleen & Whitney Cerak
with Mark Tabb

HOWARD BOOKS
A DIVISION OF SIMON & SCHUSTER
New York   London   Toronto   Sydney

HOWARD
BOOKS

Published by Howard Books, a division of Simon & Schuster, Inc.
1230 Avenue of the Americas, New York, NY 10020
www.howardpublishing.com

Mistaken Identity © 2008 Don & Susie Van Ryn and
Newell, Colleen & Whitney Cerak

Published in association with Ambassador Literary Agency, Nashville, Tennessee.

Library of Congress Cataloging-in-Publication Data is available upon request

ISBN: 978-1-84737-382-3

10 9 8 7 6 5 4 3 2

HOWARD and colophon are registered trademarks of Simon & Schuster, Inc.

Printed and bound in Australia by Griffin Press

For information regarding special discounts for bulk purchases,
please contact: Simon & Schuster Special Sales at 1-800-456-6798
or business@simonandschuster.com.

Interior design by Jaime Putorti

CONTENTS

Contents

PROLOGUE

We have been hesitant to write this book. As you will soon discover, this story is not as simple as it appears. It involves more than our two families and a bizarre case of mistaken identity. While many people were indirectly impacted by the events you are about to read, seven families other than our own were directly and tragically impacted. Four of those families suffered and continue to suffer from the loss of their precious loved ones: the families of Laurel Erb, Brad Larson, Betsy Smith, and Monica Felver. Three individuals—Connie Magers, Vickie Rhodes, and Michelle Miller—all staff members at Taylor University, lived through the horrible moments of April 26, 2006, and their lives will never be the same.

Out of respect to these people and many others, we chose not to write a blow-by-blow account of all that happened on the night of the accident. Nor do we want to give the impression that our story somehow supersedes those of the others involved. We are keenly aware that the only reason our story stands out is due to the unique situation surrounding the mistaken identity that thrust this story into the national spotlight. Neither of our families asked for nor enjoyed the attention we received. We're both very private families, and to have our lives thrown open before the world caused us discomfort.

We were also hesitant to write this book due to concern for Whitney herself. At the onset of her recovery and healing process, she often said she did not want to be known as "that girl." Her hope was for this all to quiet down, for a chance to be normal again. She did not want the attention.

However, in the days and months following the unique reversal of May 31, 2006, many people from around the world contacted both our families, telling us how God had used our experience to speak to their lives. As we prayed for God to help us understand the hows and the whys around these events, our hearts became open to sharing this story as a way to encourage others. At the one-year memorial of the accident, our two families sat down together for breakfast and immediately felt a kindred spirit. At that time, Whitney shared how she was beginning to see how God could use this story for greater good. As we talked, we sensed that the time was right to share what you are about to read.

In the discussions that followed, we wrestled with the right approach to telling this story. Many people played a part in this drama, each with a unique perspective and their own story to tell. Finding a way to blend so many voices proved to be a daunting task. Finally, we settled upon simply writing the book from the vantage point of each family, describing the events as they unfolded around us. In order to help you experience what we experienced, we've re-created the events and conversations. In order to keep the story moving, we at times chose to combine events that took place over several days into one event. To protect the privacy of those involved, we often use only first names, or on rare occasions, names have been changed. However, none of the events within this story have been enhanced or over-dramatized. We actually lived through everything you are about to read.

It is a horrible thing to lose a child. Yet even in the midst of the worst of tragedies, God reveals Himself. These are not just words we use to keep our spirits up during difficult days. We have experienced this revelation for ourselves. Above all things, this is the message we hope to convey. This is a story about God's grace and His love for us that transcends the worst this world can dish out.

None of us are in any way unique or special. We are simply average people who have accepted God's love for us, demonstrated through Jesus Christ's death and resurrection. God has proven Himself faithful to each of us, giving comfort and strength when in our humanness we were in great need. And His faithfulness has deepened our trust in Him.

The story of how two girls, Laura Van Ryn and Whitney Cerak, could be mistaken for each other may seem fantastic and unbelievable, yet that's not the real story here. This book is really about how God has sustained two families through His grace.

We hope after all that is said on these pages, you see it is really all about Him.

MISTAKEN IDENTITY

I

THE EXCHANGE

Colleen Cerak woke up with a start to the sound of the phone ringing. Her eyes could barely focus as she tried to make out the alarm clock on the nightstand. It was nearly two in the morning, Wednesday, May 31. When she finally reached the phone, she thought she recognized the voice on the other end as a man identified himself as the Grant County coroner. The same man had called five weeks earlier, telling her that Whitney, her eighteen-year-old daughter, had died in an accident along with three other Taylor University students and a university employee. That call also came late at night. *Why would the coroner call me in the middle of the night now?* she wondered.

"The county chaplain is monitoring this call," the coroner told her. Then he asked what struck Colleen as a very strange question. "Are you alone?"

"What? Yes. I mean no," she said. "Carly, my daughter, is home with me."

"Would you please ask her to listen in on this conversation?"

If she hadn't been so asleep, Colleen might have asked why it mattered if she were alone, and why the coroner had called at such an ungodly hour. But she didn't. Her body was awake, but her mind hadn't caught up with it yet. She climbed out of bed, walked across the hall to Carly's room, and woke her up. "I need you to listen in on this call. I'm going downstairs to get the other phone. Don't hang up," Colleen said.

Carly was sound asleep when her mother threw the cordless phone on her bed. "What? You want me to do what? Why?" Carly asked, but Colleen had already started down the stairs. Half asleep, but already panicking, Carly put the phone to her ear. She listened as her mother asked the man to identify himself again. The moment she heard him say he was the coroner, Carly felt sick to her stomach.

"We now know," the coroner said, "that the accident survivor in the hospital identified as Laura Van Ryn is not in fact Laura. This fact was confirmed earlier this evening through her dental records."

Carly listened upstairs while Colleen was downstairs on the main extension. Neither of them said a word, their minds unable to comprehend what they were hearing. Then the coroner dropped his bombshell. "We have reason to believe your daughter may be alive."

"No. No. That's impossible. We buried her," Colleen said. In her half-awake state, she thought the coroner was saying that

Whitney had been alive when she was placed in her casket, meaning the family had buried her alive. The thought horrified her. The coroner quickly clarified what he meant. "We have reason to believe that the girl identified as Laura Van Ryn is, in fact, your daughter Whitney Cerak."

The moment Carly heard the coroner say that Laura was Whitney, she threw down the phone and stormed down the stairs. "No, no, no!" she screamed. "Hang up the phone, Mom. HANG UP! I can't believe someone would be so cruel as to pull a prank like this. This is the worst thing I've ever heard of IN MY LIFE!"

"What did you say?" Colleen said to the coroner. She could hardly hear his response.

"Mom, listen to me!" Carly yelled. "There's no way that isn't Laura. Her family and her boyfriend have been right at her side for five weeks. *Five weeks!* Don't you think they would have noticed if it weren't Laura? A lot of my friends have seen her. Kelly was there! Mom, don't you think *my own roommate* would have noticed something as obvious as this!? Whitney doesn't look like Laura. Why would someone do this?" She began crying. "Mom, hang up the phone. Hang up, HANG UP!"

Finally Colleen asked the coroner, "May I call you back? I really need some time to think."

The coroner seemed taken aback by her question. "Mrs. Cerak, this is a very serious matter. We need you to bring your daughter's dental records to the hospital in Grand Rapids as quickly as possible so that we can make a positive identification."

"I understand that. What's your number there?"

"Mrs. Cerak!"

"May I please have your number?" Colleen's mind could not process what he was telling her; she was in shock. *Maybe Carly is right. Maybe this is nothing but a cruel, cruel hoax.* Once Colleen had the phone number, she hung up the phone and sank into her chair. Carly sat across from her on the sofa, fuming.

"Who could be so cruel?" Carly asked. Colleen didn't respond. She checked the phone number and discovered that the call had, in fact, come from Marion General Hospital in Indiana, the hospital to which Whitney's body had been taken on the night she died.

"That doesn't mean the call was real," Carly protested. She looked over at her mother. "Mom, you don't actually believe this garbage, do you?" She threw up her hands in frustration. In her mind, Carly believed she had to be the voice of reason in the family. Her father, a youth pastor, was in New York with a group of high school seniors for their annual graduation trip. With him gone, she kicked into full big-sister mode. "Mom, believe me. I *know* that the girl in the hospital is Laura, not Whitney. I know what I'm talking about. Who are you going to believe, your own daughter or some stranger making prank calls in the middle of the night!?"

Colleen didn't know what to do next. She hesitated to call and awaken her husband, Newell, when she didn't yet have any firm information. Going on this trip had been a hard enough decision for him. It was his first step toward something approaching normalcy in his job since they'd lost Whitney five weeks earlier. If this was in fact a hoax, Colleen saw no reason to make him suffer through it as well. Unsure of where else to turn, she called Newell's best friend and coworker, Pastor Jim Mathis, who had walked with the family through the tragedy of Whitney's death. "Jim, we have a situation here," she said, "and I don't know where else to turn. We just received a phone call . . ."

"A fake phone call!" Carly shouted in the background.

"We just received a phone call from someone claiming to be the Grant County coroner. He said . . ."—Colleen could hardly believe the words were coming out of her mouth—"he said that Whitney may be alive."

"What?" Jim said. "How?"

"I don't know. I don't even know if the call was real. Would you check it out for me? I don't think I can."

"Sure. What's the number?"

Five minutes later he called back and said, "It looks like we need to go on another road trip."

As soon as she hung up the phone, Colleen called the family dentist for Whitney's dental records, which he said he would bring over right away. Only then did she call her husband. The moment Colleen said his name, Newell knew something was wrong. "Not Carly," he said. "Please tell me that it's not Carly." With Whitney gone, he couldn't bear the thought of something happening to their only surviving daughter.

"No, no, no. Carly's fine. It's uh . . . it's about Whitney."

"What?"

"I just got a call from the Grant County coroner's office, and they think . . . they think Whitney may be alive."

"That's impossible," he said. "We buried her. She can't be alive."

"Let me talk to him," Carly yelled in the background and then grabbed the phone out of her mother's hand. "Don't believe any of this, Dad. The phone call said they think Laura is Whitney, but she can't be. My friends saw her. They know Whitney. Believe me, Dad, this is impossible!"

"I know, Carly. I know" was all he could say in response.

Colleen got back on the line. "Jim is going to drive us down to Grand Rapids so we can hand over Whitney's dental records to the hospital. I'm sure it's nothing but a wild-goose chase, but we have to go."

"Be sure to call me as soon as you get there," Newell said. Then he hung up the phone and tried to sleep, to no avail. His mind spun out of control as he lay in the dark. He replayed all that had happened since Colleen had first called him on April 26, 2006, and told him that Whitney had been in an accident. He had been away on a ministry-related trip that night as well. Since then he'd carried a hole in his soul that could not be filled. Yet it wasn't a grief without hope. He knew beyond a shadow of a doubt that Whitney was in the very presence of God in heaven. Yet now the family was told she was not in heaven, but alive in a hospital in Grand Rapids, Michigan. "Unbelievable," he repeated over and over.

As he tossed and turned in his bed, one thought raced through his mind: *How can this even be possible?* If a mistake had been made, someone would have noticed in the first couple of days. But five weeks? *Five weeks?!* Impossible. How could the Van Ryns not have realized this girl wasn't their daughter? She must be horribly disfigured, since it wasn't just the immediate family who would have to be mistaken. Her boyfriend and all of Laura's closest friends had also visited her in the hospital, and not one of them had alerted authorities that there might be a mistake. How could no one have noticed they had misidentified the person in that bed?

Neither he nor Colleen had seen Whitney's body after the accident. It had made sense at the time, but now a wave of self-doubt washed over him. *We didn't want the image of Whit lying in a casket burned in our minds,* he reminded himself. *Colleen and I agreed that we didn't want that to be the first thing we thought of when we thought about her.* Not once had they questioned their decision. Now, for the first time, Newell wondered how the authorities had identified the bodies at the scene of the accident. That opened the door for the biggest question of all: Could Whitney really be alive?

While Newell tossed and turned in bed at a campground in New Jersey, the rest of the family got ready for what Carly later called "the worst car trip of my life." Colleen told her, "You should pack some clothes to take with us. If this really is Whitney, we'll probably stay down there for a while."

Carly shot her mother a look. "Would you be realistic, Mother? I told you. My friends have been down there. They've seen her. They all know it's Laura. If it were Whitney, don't you think Laura's *best friends* would have noticed?"

"Carly, please, we just have to make sure. Okay?" Colleen said.

"We already know for sure," Carly said and stormed off. She refused to entertain even the slightest hope that her sister could be alive. If she did, and those hopes were crushed, it would feel like the night Whitney died all over again.

Colleen went downstairs and woke up Sandra, whom the family lovingly called, "the girl who lives in the basement." Sandra Sepulveda had moved in with the Ceraks during her sophomore year of high school after her family moved away from Gaylord. With time she became like another sister to Carly and Whitney. Colleen shook her and said, "Sandra, we've got to drive down to Grand Rapids. Right now. Tonight."

"What? Why?" Sandra said, still half asleep.

"The coroner called and told us Whitney may be alive," Colleen said. The words struck her as absurd even as they left her lips.

"*What? How?*" Sandra yelled as she jumped out of bed and raced up the stairs after Colleen.

"We don't know. That's why we have to go to GR," Colleen said. Sandra peppered her with questions, but all Colleen could say in response was, "I've already told you everything I know."

Colleen, Carly, and Sandra climbed in Jim's car and drove toward Grand Rapids, four hours away. No one said much of anything for a very long time. Carly sat in the backseat next to Sandra, still fuming. Finally she said, "What will the Van Ryns think when we come barging into Laura's room?"

"They aren't there," Colleen said. "I was told they left the hospital some time on Tuesday after the hospital confirmed the girl in the room wasn't Laura."

"What?" Carly's head spun. "None of this makes any sense. There's no way they could have gone this long thinking it was Laura if it wasn't her. *No way*." No one argued her point.

Silence filled the car for the next hour. By this time Carly had cooled off. Although she didn't want to talk about it, she'd spent that hour considering the news that the Van Ryns had ended their constant vigil. *They haven't left Laura's side for five weeks. Why would they leave now? What if . . . ?* "Did they tell you why the Van Ryns left?" Carly asked, as if the earlier conversation had never ended.

"All they told me was the hospital now knows the girl in the room isn't Laura," Colleen said. "The Van Ryns left the hospital after dental records confirmed this fact. If it was Laura, they would still be there."

"That still doesn't mean that it's Whitney," Carly protested. "I can't believe it's not Laura, but if it isn't, it could be some random girl they put in her room by mistake." Even as she said the words, she realized how foolish they sounded. Carly didn't want to admit it, but she, too, had started to believe Whitney might be alive.

Colleen told the girls, "You know if Whitney is alive, Hollywood will have to make this into a movie." Everyone laughed, even Carly.

"And, if they do, Jennifer Lopez will have to play Sandra," Colleen joked. "After all, they're both Puerto Rican."

"I think Robert Redford will have to be Newell," Colleen said.

"Watch it, Mom. We know how you feel about Robert Redford," Carly joked.

"Stop it," Colleen laughed. "They'd have to have Kate Hudson play Whitney. I've always thought they kind of looked alike,"

Colleen said. "And Mel Gibson for you, Jim." Everyone roared with laughter when she said that.

Colleen, Carly, Sandra, and Jim pulled into the parking lot of Spectrum Health Continuing Care Hospital around seven in the morning. Two hospital employees met them and tried to explain the situation and then asked if the Ceraks had any questions. They had only one: Where is she? As the women led them down the hall, Carly began to shake uncontrollably. She could hardly breathe. Colleen led the way, with Carly and Sandra hanging on behind. Jim respectfully lagged back several steps.

When they reached the room with the nameplate "Laura Van Ryn," Colleen took a deep breath and pushed the door open slightly. Although the lights in the room were dim, there was no mistaking the girl lying on the hospital bed. Colleen let out a sigh of relief and whispered. "It's Whitney."

Carly lunged past her mother and rushed to her sister, with Sandra and Colleen close behind. The three of them started hugging Whitney and burst into tears. It really was her. Her blonde hair, her blue eyes, her nose, and the shape of her mouth; beyond a shadow of a doubt, it was Whitney!

Whitney slowly opened her eyes, wide and expressionless. Although her neck brace restricted her movement, she nodded her head yes over and over as her sister and mother repeated her name. Carly fell to the floor sobbing, her body unable to contain her overwhelming joy. The women who had escorted the Ceraks to Whitney's room rushed in and tried to quiet the three of them down. "She can't handle this much stimulation," they said.

"But my sister is alive. My sister is *alive*!" Carly said and the celebration continued.

Colleen pulled out her cell phone. She could barely see the numbers due to the tears in her eyes. "Newell," she said, "I'm standing here and it's Whitney. It really is Whitney."

Newell could not believe what he was hearing. He thought he must be dreaming. "Hang up the phone and call me right back," he said, just to make sure this was real. Immediately his cell phone rang again. "I'm standing here and she's as beautiful as ever," Colleen said. Newell fell to his knees, crying like a baby.

"What does she look like?" he asked. "Is anything wrong with her?"

"No." Colleen replied. "There's not a mark on her face. It's really her."

Then Newell heard a sound he thought he would never hear again. Through the phone he heard the daughter he believed he'd said good-bye to for the final time five weeks earlier say in almost a whisper, "I love you, Dad."

2

APRIL 26, 2006

Carly. It's sista. I signed you up for global commute night and I think a few of my friends are coming too, like Amy, Ann, and maybe Emily, but that doesn't mean I don't want you to come, I totally do. And are you working the banquet in Fort Wayne? I hope you are, I hope you are, I hope you are! K. Love you. Bye.

VOICE-MAIL MESSAGE FROM WHITNEY LEFT ON CARLY'S CELL PHONE, WEDNESDAY, APRIL 26, 2006

Lisa Van Ryn sat upstairs in her parents' home in Caledonia, Michigan, watching television and talking on the phone to her friend Julie. The two became friends as teenagers when they met at a camp in Michigan's Upper Peninsula. Later they served on staff there, along with Lisa's sister Laura and another friend, Brad Larson.

While Julie talked to Lisa on the home phone, she was also exchanging text messages on her cell phone with Laura and Brad. The two were sitting next to each other in a Taylor University van on their way back to the Upland campus from Taylor's campus in Fort Wayne. That evening Laura and Brad had worked at a banquet there honoring Taylor's new president.

"Okay, okay, this one is great," Julie told Lisa.

"Why? What did they say?"

"Get this. They both sent me the same text at the exact same time. It says, 'It's your choice who you text back first.' "

Lisa laughed. "That's great. So the one you like most, you text first? Very funny. So which one will you choose?"

"I don't know. Which would you choose?" Julie said. "Oh, wait. That's a stupid question. Of course you would pick your sister. All right, hold on while I reply." Julie sent text messages back to both, but she didn't tell Lisa who she replied to first. Neither Laura nor Brad responded to Julie's texts.

Downstairs, the thought of calling Laura flashed through Don Van Ryn's mind. He'd just arrived home from an exceptionally long workday at a trade show in Detroit. It had been a good day made better by the fact that Laura's boyfriend, Aryn Linenger, had been able to meet Don at the trade show during lunch. Aryn wasn't just a boyfriend. Don and Susie knew that he was planning to ask Laura to marry him when she graduated from Taylor in three weeks. The two met when she was a freshman and he a senior and had dated ever since. Don and Susie had already started thinking of Aryn as a son-in-law, which made Don enjoy spending time with him.

While Don and Aryn walked through the trade show floor together, Aryn's cell phone rang. It was Laura. The two talked briefly; then Aryn asked Don, "Would you like to say hi to Laura?" Expecting to hear his daughter's voice, Don took the phone and said, "Hi, Laurie." No answer. He repeated his greeting, but the call had dropped. "Oh well," he told Aryn as he handed him back his phone, "I'll talk to her later." It was later now, but Don was too tired to do anything except kick off his shoes and collapse into his favorite chair.

Susie had not been home much longer than Don. Wednesdays can be long days at the hair salon where she worked, and she had run a few errands on the way home. She tried calling Laura sometime between eight and eight-thirty, but the call went straight to voice mail. Susie didn't think much of it. She planned to try again when she got home, but the evening got away from her.

Around ten the home phone rang. When Susie answered, a man on the other end asked, "Is this the Van Ryn household?" Susie thought it was some sort of sales call, although most telemarketers didn't call this late. He went on to identify himself as the chaplain of the Parkview Hospital in Fort Wayne. "Your daughter has been brought here as a patient," he said. "She was involved in a very serious accident earlier this evening. She is in critical but stable condition."

Fort Wayne? What is Laura doing in Fort Wayne? Susie struggled to make sense of what she'd just been told.

Don could tell by the look on his wife's face that something had happened to one of their children. He picked up the extension in time to hear the chaplain say that Laura was unconscious in the intensive care unit. She had several broken bones and a very serious head injury. Don felt his body go numb.

Susie looked at him, her eyes wide as the color drained from her face. Laura was the youngest of their four fiercely independent children. Any one of them would jump in a car and drive anywhere and everywhere and never think a thing about it. Susie prayed for their safety every day, yet she wasn't prepared for a phone call like this. Her pulse quickened, and she found it hard to breathe. "Can you repeat that for me?" she said.

"Your daughter Laura has been seriously injured in an automobile accident. She is in critical condition and unconscious. However, she's stable and in intensive care," the chaplain repeated.

Don's first instinct was to drop everything and head straight for Fort Wayne. "Where exactly is the hospital?" Don asked. "We are on our way."

Susie went upstairs to Lisa's room. "Laura's been in an accident," she said. "Your dad and I are going to drive down to Fort Wayne. If you want to come with us we're going to leave in about ten minutes."

If I want to come with you? Of course I want to go with you, Lisa thought. She threw her toothbrush and Bible into her backpack, and grabbed a sweatshirt and her cell phone. Nothing else. Before she left she called a friend to ask her to cover her shift the next day at the Olive Garden. She thought she would be back at work in a couple of days. Neither she nor her parents had any idea of the ordeal that lay ahead of them.

Don, Susie, and Lisa jumped into their car and headed south toward Fort Wayne. As it turned out, Lisa had packed more than either of her parents. Not one of them were thinking of what they might need for an extended stay out of town. All they knew was that Laura had been in an accident, and they wanted to get to her as quickly as possible.

Before they'd even reached the on-ramp of I-96, Don began dialing Aryn's number. *Hi, this is Aryn. I can't get to the phone*

right now. Leave me a message and I will get back with you.
"Aryn, this is Don. I need you to call me on my cell right away."
He hung up his phone and immediately tried Aryn's home number. No answer there either.

"Why don't you try Jim and Trixie," Susie said. "They may know where he is."

"That's a good idea," Don said. He dialed Aryn's parents' home number. "Jim, Don Van Ryn here. I'm trying to get hold of Aryn. He isn't there with you, is he . . . Do you know where he may be? . . . Well, listen, we just received a call that Laura's been in an accident down in Indiana. Suz, Lisa, and I are on our way down to Parkview Hospital in Fort Wayne. We don't know much right now, just that she's in critical condition in ICU . . . Yeah . . . They-said the van she was in was hit by a truck, but they didn't tell us much more than that."

While Don tried to locate Aryn, Lisa sat in the backseat tracking down her brothers, Kenny and Mark. Kenny was staying with a friend in Chicago for the week, while Mark was in school at Northern Michigan University in Marquette. In between calls to them, her cell rang. "Hi, Dawn . . . No, we don't know anything either. What have you heard? Have they released any of the other names? If we hear anything I'll call." After she hung up, she said, "That was Dawn, Brad's sister. She's really upset."

"Which hospital did they take Brad to?" Susie asked.

"She doesn't know. They haven't been told anything yet," Lisa said.

A sick feeling washed over Susie. "Oh no," she said. "I don't like the sound of that at all."

About that time Don's cell phone rang. He didn't recognize the number. "Don Van Ryn here," he said. He then listened for a few moments before saying, "Suz, it's the hospital. They want to insert a device into Laura's skull to monitor the pressure on her brain, but they need our permission before they can do it."

"Of course. Whatever they need to do." Susie's voice cracked as the words came out. *Oh, God,* she prayed, *what will we find when we get there?*

Although she felt the crunch that every college student feels in the last few weeks of a semester, Carly decided to skip studying Wednesday evening to play tennis with her friend Terra. The papers and assignments could wait one more day. Carly didn't care that much about tennis, but Terra was dealing with a family tragedy and she needed a friend. Swatting a ball around the tennis courts that sit next to Taylor University's Rediger Chapel seemed to Carly to be the perfect way to get her friend's mind off all she was going through, if only for an hour or two. The match wasn't too competitive as they talked about school and friends and their plans after college. One subject did not come up: the specifics of what Terra and her family were going through. That had been Carly's plan all along. She wasn't dodging the topic, but this perfect Indiana spring night didn't seem to be the time nor the place to talk about it. The grief would still be there after the match was over.

About halfway through their match, Carly's boyfriend, Ben, came running over from the parking lot to the tennis courts. Carly thought he wanted to take on the winner, but then she noticed the look on his face. "You need to call Whitney right away," he said with panic in his voice. "There's been an accident with one of the Taylor vans. She might have been in it," he said.

"Was it bad?" Carly asked. Ben didn't answer. He just looked down at the ground and shuffled his feet.

Carly felt the hair on the back of her neck stand on end. She raced to her car, grabbed her cell phone, and dialed Whitney's number. After several rings the call went to voice mail. Carly hung up and dialed again. No answer, only voice mail. She dialed again. And again. And again. No answer. "How did you find out about this?" she asked Ben.

"It's on the news and it's already all over campus," he said.

With that Carly jumped in her car, shouted for Ben and Terra to get in, and drove across campus to Olson Hall, the dorm where Whitney lived. If anyone knew exactly what had happened, it would be Shelley, Olson's head resident. But Shelley was nowhere to be found. As word of the accident spread, more and more students came into Olson. Most were crying, which made Carly angry. She didn't want anyone crying over Whitney because she refused to believe Whitney had been hurt in the accident. For all she knew, her sister hadn't even been in the Taylor van involved in the accident, since the students working that night's banquet in Fort Wayne were riding back in two vans. And even if Whitney had been in the accident, no one really knew how badly anyone had been hurt.

Carly walked outside onto the lawn in front of Olson and dialed her home number. No answer and no voice mail. She called her father's cell phone. He didn't answer either. *They must be talking to each other*, Carly thought. "Argh! Switch over," she said as she reached her father's voice mail once again. She kept pressing redial, hoping she would eventually get through to one number or the other.

"So did you get a lot of work done today?" Colleen asked Newell. They'd been on the phone for about ten minutes. He had gone to Mississippi with a group of men and women from his community to rebuild houses destroyed by Hurricane Katrina. Around 350 volunteers had come together from across the country to work with Habitat for Humanity on the project.

"Yeah, quite a bit, considering how hot it is down here. I can't believe it's like this in April. I would hate to be down here in the middle of the summer." Newell's phone beeped with an incoming call; he ignored it. "How did your Bible study go with the girls tonight?"

"Really well," Colleen said. "We had a great prayer time. The girls opened up more than usual." The call waiting beeped in her ear. "Now my phone's beeping."

"It has to be Carly or Whitney. No one else would be this persistent," Newell said. "You want to switch over?"

"I'll call them right back. I haven't talked to you all day. I miss you. I'm ready for you to get home."

"Me too. Okay, my phone's beeping again. Maybe I should take it," Newell said.

"Switch over and find out what she wants. I'll hold," Colleen said. He did but missed the call.

"Now mine's beeping. I'll call you back," Colleen said. She pressed the Flash button on the phone. "Hello."

"Mom," Carly said. The desperation in Carly's voice told Colleen that something was wrong. "There's been an accident at Taylor with one of the vans," Carly continued. "No one is sure if Whitney was in the van or not. You need to pray for her. Please pray." Colleen wanted more details, but there were none to be had. "There's a prayer service in the chapel in ten minutes. Maybe they'll give more details then. I'll call you back as soon as I know something," Carly said, then hung up and called her dad. She gave him the same report she'd given her mother. When she hung up, her phone immediately started ringing. One friend after another called. She didn't answer.

When Carly, Ben, and Terra walked into Rediger Chapel for the prayer vigil, it was already packed with students. Most were sobbing. Carly went up to the balcony so that she wouldn't have to talk to anyone. She felt as if she were in a different world. Her friends surrounded her, all of them crying. Again, she wouldn't let herself give in to tears, although her body shook with fear. She still wanted to believe her sister was all right.

After what felt like an eternity, a Taylor official walked up to the podium and announced that earlier that evening, a northbound semitrailer crossed over the center median of I-69 and struck a southbound fifteen-passenger Taylor University van near the Marion exit. The van was carrying five students and four food services employees. Of the nine people in the van, five had died. The names would not be released until all of the parents had been notified. Throughout the chapel, people began moaning and wailing. Carly felt her heart drop. The official went on to explain that two survivors had been airlifted to Parkview Hospital in Fort Wayne, one of whom was in critical condition. The rest of the victims had been taken to Marion General Hospital, about fifteen miles from the Taylor campus.

Carly jumped up and ran out of the building. She had to get to Marion immediately. No one had been able to give her any information regarding Whitney. Since the five bodies and two of the survivors had been taken to Marion General, it seemed like the logical (and closest) place to find answers.

During the ride to the hospital, Carly and her friends pleaded with God for Whitney's life. Carly found it nearly impossible to pray beyond the words *Please, God, give me my sister.* She repeated this plea over and over again. Carly's friends were sobbing, but she did not cry. *No, I can't cry,* she told herself. *If I give in to tears, that means giving in to my worst fears. I will not do that. Whitney is one of the survivors. She has to be.*

They pulled into the hospital parking lot and ran toward the door. A crowd had already gathered in the front lobby when Carly approached the information desk. "I was told they brought my sister here. Whitney Cerak. Can you tell me what room she's in and how she's doing?" Carly asked.

The front desk worker scrolled through the pages on her computer. "I'm sorry, miss, I don't have any information on your sister."

"But she was in the Taylor van accident. I was told they brought the people from the accident here."

"That is correct. But I can't give out any specific information about who is here or anything about their conditions."

"So who can tell me?" Carly said, her frustration rising. A nurse walked over.

"Did I hear you say you are a family member of one of the Taylor accident victims?" she asked.

"Yes," Carly said.

"If you like, you can wait in the chapel. As soon as we have more information, someone will come in there and give it to you." The nurse then directed Carly and her friends down the hall to the chapel. There they waited. And waited. And waited.

Back in Gaylord, Michigan, Colleen was frantic for more information. Knowing she needed to keep the phone line open, she made only one call. "Bob," she said to her friend Bob Scott, a man who she knew she could count on to pray intently for her situation, "Whitney's been in an accident, and we don't know if she is okay. Would you please pray for us?" Bob assured her that he would.

Then she sat down and began pleading with God herself. As she prayed, Terra's parents, who also lived in the area, walked into her living room and began praying as well. Soon Jim Mathis joined them. As time dragged by and the phone did not ring, Colleen used a cell phone to call some old friends in Upland, thinking that perhaps the local media had released more information. No one knew anything more. County officials still had not released any names.

Finally Colleen tried one last possible connection in Indiana, but no one answered her call. As soon as she hung up her cell phone, the house phone rang. Colleen swallowed hard before pressing the talk button. "Hello," she said.

"May I speak with Newell or Colleen Cerak?"

"This is Colleen."

The man then identified himself as the Grant County chaplain. "I am sorry," he said, "but your daughter Whitney was in an accident this evening. She was pronounced dead at the scene."

Colleen went numb. Tears began pouring down her face. "What . . . uh . . . is there anything I need to do?" Seeing her distress, her friends knew the worst had happened, and immediately went to Colleen and wrapped their arms around her.

"We need you and your husband to come here to make arrangements for your daughter's body to be taken back home. I'm very sorry to have to tell you this. I am so sorry for your loss," the chaplain said.

As soon as she hung up the phone, she called Newell. Her voice broke as she said, "I'm sorry. I'm so sorry." She could hardly force the words out. "Whitney's gone," she said.

"No. No, Colleen," Newell said, his voice cracking.

"She's gone, Newell," Colleen said again. "They pronounced her dead at the accident." The two of them broke down together on the phone.

When Newell hung up, his Mississippi coworkers surrounded him. They wrapped their arms around him and began praying. "No. No. Not Whitney" was all Newell could say.

Carly sat with her friends in the chapel at the Marion General Hospital. More and more students started arriving at the hospital.

No one knew anything more than the brief bit of information given at Rediger Chapel earlier that evening. Finally Carly's cell phone rang. She walked out into the hall to take the call, with Ben following her. Jim Mathis was on the other end. Colleen had barely been able to muster the strength to call Newell. Knowing she couldn't wait until she could pull herself together to tell Carly the news, she asked Jim to call her daughter for her. As soon as Carly heard his voice, she knew the news was bad. She heard the sound of people crying in the background. When Jim told her that Whitney didn't make it, Carly collapsed, screaming and crying. Ben kicked a chair in anger and cried out in anguish. Her friends rushed out into the hall and embraced her. They gently lifted her back onto her feet and carried her back into the chapel.

The hospital staff arranged for Carly and her friends to stay in a room where they could escape the crowd of students and media. Officials came back with questions about Whitney. They wanted to know her age, birth date, the kind of information one finds in an obituary. Later someone brought Whitney's purse and the few other belongings found at the accident scene to Carly. They reeked of diesel fuel. Carly pushed them away and broke down further. As she sat sobbing, a thought pierced her mind. *Okay, Carly, here is the big test. Do you love God even though your sister is dead?* She looked up at her friends, tears running down her face. "God is still good," she said. "This accident didn't change that *at all.*"

Carly's phone rang again. She glanced at the caller ID screen and saw the word *Dad.* As she flipped open her phone, she went out into the hall where she could be alone. No one followed. She ran to the end of the hallway and pressed the phone against her ear. At the sound of her father's voice she fell against a wall and cried like she'd never cried in her life. Her body ached and awful moans came pouring out. "Dad . . . *nooooooo*," she wailed into her phone. "No, Dad, Whitney can't be gone. She is my best friend."

3

ICU

Wed., April 26

Oh, Laurie, that was a phone call I never wanted to have. I can't explain my feelings—dread, fear, anxiety, immediate pleading with God to spare your life, thankful that you were still alive, disbelief like I was in a dream. The ride to Fort Wayne was *long*. Many phone calls. People caring, praying, loving you from the very beginning. We (Lisa, Dad, and I) got here about 1:15 A.M. Were met by several friends of yours from TU. When they brought us in to see you, honey, my heart was so full of love for you. To see my sweet sunshine girl hooked up to tubes was almost more than I could bear. It amazes me that God has such strength when I am so weak. Only He could uphold me as He has. Aryn, Jim, and Trixie were here a couple of hours after us. Aryn was in rough shape. He loves you so much. So do I, sweet Laurie.

FROM SUSIE'S PRAYER JOURNAL

"You need to be prepared for what you will see when you walk into her room," the doctor said to Don, Susie, and Lisa as they stood in the hall just outside the intensive care unit. "Laura was thrown some fifty feet in a very violent accident. Her face is swollen and scratched and bruised. And she is on a respirator. She was breathing on her own when the paramedics got to her, but we feel that it is best to let the respirator do the hard work of breathing so that her body can concentrate on healing itself."

"But she's going to make it, right?" Don asked. Susie leaned close to him and squeezed his arm.

"Your daughter is in critical condition. We're still working to assess the full extent of her injuries. Right now, I would say her chances are somewhat promising. But she isn't going to go walking out of here any time soon. She has several broken bones, including a shattered elbow and a badly broken leg, along with a broken collarbone. We're most concerned about her brain injury. We can't just take an X-ray and tell how extensive it may be. That's why when you go in to see her, you'll see a tube coming up out of her skull. Don't be alarmed. That's the pressure-monitoring device we called you about earlier this evening." The doctor paused for a moment, then asked, "Do you have any questions?"

Don, Susie, and Lisa looked at one another, trying to process what they'd just been told. Although they knew Laura was seriously injured, they had not known what to expect when they arrived at the hospital. Susie looked up at Don, tears running down her face. Don pulled her close. Finally, Lisa spoke up. "Can we see her now?"

"Not yet, but soon," the doctor said. "We're still working on getting her settled in. A nurse will come and get you when she's ready. Again, I want you to be prepared. She's not going to look like herself." Don glanced at his watch. It was nearly two in the morning; the accident had occurred over five hours ago. *What else could they be doing?* he wondered. *How bad is this?*

As instructed, Don, Susie, and Lisa walked over to the ICU

waiting area, which by this time had also filled with Laura's friends from Taylor. As the Van Ryns walked in, all eyes were on them. Laura's roommates hugged Susie and Lisa. Wynn Lembright and Skip Trudeau, two administrators from Taylor, were also there. "How is she?" Wynn asked.

"She's hanging in there," Don said.

"Good. A lot of people are praying for her," Wynn said.

"I know, I know," Don said, his mind spinning as it tried to process what he'd just been told by the doctor. "The lobby was filled with students when we walked in. They told us about the prayer service at Taylor tonight."

"Any word on the others from the accident?" Lisa asked.

Wynn and Skip looked at each other. "Laura's one of four survivors," Skip said, "although the other three were not as seriously injured."

"What about Brad Larson?" Don asked.

Winn and Skip looked at each other again. "We can go ahead and tell them, since the formal announcement will come soon at the university," Wynn said. He paused before continuing, "Brad didn't make it. He died in the accident along with staff member Monica Felver and students Laurel Erb, Betsy Smith, and Whitney Cerak."

"No, no, no," Lisa said as she broke into tears.

"Oh, my," Don said. He let out a long sigh as he wrapped his arm around Susie. The Van Ryns felt very close to Brad and his sister, Dawn, who had called Lisa during their drive down from Caledonia. Both Brad and Dawn had worked with the Van Ryns as counselors at the Upper Peninsula Bible Camp.

The students in the waiting area overheard Wynn telling the Van Ryns that Brad, Laurel, Betsy, Whitney, and Monica had died in the accident. Their tears and moans echoed throughout the room.

Laura's ICU room was very dark when Don, Susie, and Lisa walked in. Brain injury patients require dim lights and low stimulation to let the healing process take place. Monitors with blinking numbers and squiggly lines sat on either side of Laura's bed, each one emitting beeps that, in the quiet of the room, sounded much louder than they actually were. Though the lights were dim, they could see Laura's expressionless face poking through the white bandages that enveloped her head. "It looks like toothache bandages," Don blurted out.

None of them really knew what to say. Although Laura's face was indeed swollen with cuts and bruises, her blonde hair stuck up from the bandages, and her nose, mouth, and other features were still the same, still Laura. A ventilator tube held down by tape went into the side of her mouth. A "spike," the brain pressure monitor tube, came up and out the top right of her head, just above her forehead. In addition, IV lines and monitor cables were attached to both sides of her body.

Susie moved to Laura's side. The beeping of the machines and the *woosh* of the ventilator made her heart stand still. "Oh, Laurie," she whispered as she reached down and took hold of her daughter's hands. Tears flowed. "We're here . . . we're here."

"Laurie, it's Dad," Don said softly. "I don't know if you can hear us, but that's okay." He looked around the room and exhaled. Rather than feeling panic or fear, a sense of peace washed over

Don. "You're going to be okay," he said. "Hang in there and keep fighting. I know you're going to be okay."

Lisa simply walked over and put her arm around her mother. As she did, Susie prayed silently, *As hard as it is, God, I trust you. Laura's in your hands . . . She's in your hands.* Lisa rubbed her mother's back, just to let her know she was there. *God, I know you have a plan for Laura's life,* Susie continued praying, *it can't end here. I just know that it can't end here.*

A nurse walked into the room and began adjusting one of the monitors. "Suz," Don said, "we need to let her rest." Susie looked at him with an expression that made it clear that she didn't want to let go of Laura's hand. "It's all right," he said, "she's in good hands." The nurse smiled, but Don wasn't just talking about the hospital staff. Although he wasn't always as positive a person as he would like to be, Don felt a strong peace from God that Laura would make a full recovery. Over the previous two months he'd found himself drawn to stories in the Bible of people like Job, who went through extreme suffering, yet found God to be faithful. *God hasn't changed,* he thought to himself. *He's still at work here.* Then Don's thoughts turned to Monica, Betsy, Laurel, Whitney, and Brad, especially Brad. He let out a long sigh. *Why us and not them, Lord? Why would our daughter survive and not one of them?*

About two hours after the Van Ryns arrived at the hospital, Aryn and his parents pulled into the hospital parking garage. Aryn's mind raced as he climbed out of the car and walked toward the entrance. Memories of Laura flashed through his head, along with the fear that he would never enjoy such moments again.

When he walked into the ICU waiting room, Don, Susie, and Lisa jumped up and wrapped their arms around him. Tears flowed. "Would you like to see her?" Don asked. Aryn took a deep breath and nodded. Don and Susie took him arm in arm and walked down the hall to Laura's room.

As they walked inside, Aryn found himself speechless. He wanted to say something, anything, to tell Laura how much he loved her, yet the words wouldn't come. Instead he stood next to her bed, watching her inhale and exhale, praying that each breath would lead to another.

Shortly after Aryn arrived, a hospital staff member walked into the ICU waiting room. "Here are Laura's things," she said as she handed Lisa a bag containing shoes and a few other personal items.

Lisa reached into the bag and pulled out the Converse All-Star shoes the hospital staff had taken off Laura's feet. "These aren't Laura's shoes," she said. Aryn took the shoe out of Lisa's hand and agreed. "I never saw her wear anything like this."

"Well, those were the ones she had on when they brought her in," the staff member said as she walked out.

As Lisa pulled the other items out of the bag, she and Aryn had the same reaction. None of it matched anything they knew Laura owned. Yet neither of them thought too much of it. "Laura was always borrowing my clothes when she lived at home," Lisa said. "I doubt if anything changed after she went off to school. I'm sure these belong to one of her roommates. It's her purse, though." Earlier in the evening the family had been told that rescue workers had found the purse up against Laura's body. They had used its contents to identify her at the scene.

"They probably just had to guess with the rest of it, though," Aryn said. "From what Wynn and Skip said about the crash scene, it sounds like stuff was scattered everywhere." He paused as a thought hit him. "How far was Laura from the van?"

"Fifty feet."

"Wow," he said softly, in almost a whisper. "It's a miracle she survived."

"Yeah," Lisa said. "It really is."

By the time Kenny and Mark arrived, the Taylor students had long since left the hospital, leaving the Van Ryns in the ICU waiting area alone with Aryn and his parents. It took Kenny a few hours to drive from Chicago, and Mark flew down from Marquette to Fort Wayne. Both walked through the door with a sense of purpose, almost as though they were on a mission. The first words out of both their mouths were "What's the latest?" No "Hi, Mom" or "Hi, Dad. Both cut right to the point.

When Kenny arrived, Don, Susie, and Lisa led him back to Laura's room in the ICU. He didn't say a word, but stood there, staring at his sister. After only a minute or two, they walked back to the waiting area. Four hours later, when Mark arrived, they took him back. He walked in, saw his sister lying there, and turned and walked out of the room, tears streaming down his face. Perhaps the worse part of the night for Don was telling his boys that Brad didn't make it. He didn't know what his family would have done if both Laura *and* Brad had died that night.

Once the five of them were all together at Parkview Hospital, Don sat them down and went over what the doctors had told them up to this point. "Here's what we know," he said. "Her leg's pretty bad and will probably need surgery at some point. Possibly the elbow as well. Their big concern is the brain injury. I guess it will be a few days before they know what we're looking at with that." Drawing from his matter-of-fact Dutch heritage, Don didn't try to sugarcoat anything they'd been told, nor did he talk much about what the days and weeks ahead might hold. He ended his update, saying, "So this is what we're dealing with. Anyone have any questions?"

No one did. They spent the rest of the night in the waiting room just outside the intensive care unit. No one got any sleep. The Van Ryns, along with Aryn and his parents, sat anxiously in the waiting room and did just that: they waited. This would prove to be the only night the family had to spend in the hospital itself. But their journey had only begun. They soon realized that they had embarked on a marathon, not a sprint. None of them had any idea where this marathon would ultimately take them. All they could do was wait and pray.

In the end, that would have to be enough.

4

COMING TO GRIPS WITH A NEW REALITY

"I can't believe this is happening," Colleen said to Jim as they headed south out of Gaylord toward Upland, Indiana. "This can't be real." Usually Colleen would fall asleep while in the car, especially during a six-hour drive in the middle of the night, but not this night. "She was just home a couple of weeks ago at Easter. She and Carly insisted on hiding Easter eggs." Colleen smiled, and then continued, "It was like they were little girls again, running around the house, laughing." Her voice broke as she said, "And now this . . . how is this possible?"

"I don't know." Jim knew he didn't need to say anything more. Colleen needed someone to listen, not try to give easy answers or empty clichés.

"I don't know if you remember this, but Whitney didn't want to go to Taylor. She wanted to buck the family tradition and go somewhere else. I guess the fact that Newell and Carly and I had all gone there only made it less attractive to her. Even though she knew we would pay for two-thirds of the cost if she went to a Christian college, and nothing if she went to a secular school, Taylor still wasn't her first choice. She applied at a state school that has a reputation for accepting almost everyone who applied. Taylor was her backup school in case the first one didn't work out. She couldn't believe it when her first choice of schools turned her down, especially since she had more than met their entry requirements. Then Taylor, which has much higher standards, accepted her. We all took it as a very clear, unmistakable sign from God that He wanted her at Taylor." Colleen's voice trailed off for a moment, then she said, "And now this. I can't help but think that if she hadn't gone to Taylor, we wouldn't be making this drive right now. But having her at Taylor was obviously part of God's plan for her life. I'm having a real hard time making sense of that."

As Colleen and Jim talked, the two became oblivious to everything else. That is, until flashing red and blue lights lit up the night behind them. They had sped through a notorious speed trap, where the speed limit on the highway drops from 65 to 55 mph. Jim pulled the car over. "If you want me to cry, I can," Colleen said. "I don't think that will be necessary," Jim replied. He asked the state trooper for permission to get out of the car, where he then explained their situation privately. A few minutes later they were back on their way without a speeding ticket.

Less than a mile before the Marion exit, they came upon the crash site. Jim slowed the car, but he did not pull over and stop. The wreckage had been cleared away hours earlier, but the scar in the median where the truck had crossed was clearly visible. Neither Colleen nor Jim said a word as tears streaked down their faces.

Even though Carly had left the hospital around four A.M. at Colleen's urging, Colleen insisted on going directly to Marion General. She needed to see the place where they'd taken Whitney after the accident. When they pulled into the hospital parking lot, it was deserted, as were the lobby and waiting rooms. The crowds of students had left hours earlier, giving the place an eerie silence. Finally Colleen found a hospital staff member and identified herself. "My daughter was one of the accident victims. Is there anything I need to do or any additional information you need from me?"

The staff member picked up the phone and made a quick call to the coroner, and then said, "No, ma'am. Everything's been taken care of. He said the identification has been done, and his office will coordinate transporting your daughter's body with the funeral home. However, if you would like to see her, we can have someone take you back."

Nausea swept over Colleen. She closed her eyes and saw an image of Whitney with an Easter basket in her hand, a huge smile on her face. Then she remembered a conversation with a friend whose teenage daughter had died the year before. *I can't shake the image of her lying in the casket,* the friend had said. Colleen knew she didn't want a similar memory of Whitney. "No," she finally answered the staff member. "I . . . uh . . ." Her voice cracked and she stopped to gather her thoughts. "Thank you, though."

After giving the staff member a number where she could be reached, Colleen and Jim left the hospital and drove to Upland, to Carly's boyfriend's house, where Carly and a group of friends had gone to try to get some rest. Sandra was also there, along with Whitney's boyfriend, Matt, and Sandra's sister, Laisa.

The house was quiet and dark when Colleen walked in. Carly, Sandra, and Ben were asleep, leaning against one another on the sofa. Colleen walked over to Carly, crouched down, and touched her arm. "Carly," she said softly. Slowly Carly opened her eyes. The moment she saw her mother she wrapped her arms around her neck and began weeping. Sandra awakened, and the three of them embraced and cried and cried. No one said a word for what felt like a very long time. There weren't any words to say.

Over the next few hours, Colleen tried to rest but couldn't. She felt too numb to sleep. *This can't be real,* she thought. *Surely I will wake up and all of this will go away. Oh, God,* she prayed. That was as far as she could get in her prayer. She knew God would fill in the rest. After tossing and turning for three hours, she got up, changed her clothes and washed her face, and then called her friend Marty Songer. "I need to go to the prayer service this morning at Taylor's chapel," she said. Marty tried telling her that she needed to rest, but Colleen wouldn't change her mind. "I've got to get out of this house and do something. Going to a place where I can be surrounded by praying people sounds like a great place to start."

When Colleen and Marty slipped into Rediger in the heart of

the Taylor campus, the service had already begun. Nearly a thousand people were packed into the chapel, but no one immediately recognized Colleen as the mother of one of the accident victims. She found a seat next to Carly's roommates, who put their arms around her without saying a word. Two rows in front of her sat Whitney's roommates, weeping.

Very few words were spoken in the first hour of the prayer service. Instead, the name of each victim flashed on the large video projection screen at the front of the chapel. Those attending prayed for the families of each victim as his or her name appeared. The names of the injured also appeared on the screen, as did the name of the truck driver who collided with the Taylor van.

WHITNEY CERAK flashed on the screen, in large white letters against a black background. Colleen stared straight ahead at Whitney's name. *It is real,* she said to herself. *Whitney is one of the five who died last night.* Up ahead, Whitney's roommates began sobbing, but Colleen couldn't cry. She waited, fully expecting her emotions to overwhelm her. Instead she felt a peace she couldn't put into words. Glancing around the auditorium, she saw hundreds of people praying. *They're praying for us. For me. For Newell. For Carly.* In that moment, she felt as though she could feel the prayers reaching up toward heaven and the arms of God physically reaching down to her in response. She closed her eyes, soaking it in.

As soon as the service ended, Jim Mathis whisked Colleen back to Ben's house. There they picked up Carly, Sandra, and Sandra's sister, Laisa. The five of them left for Indianapolis to pick up Newell at the airport. He had spent a long, sleepless night alone in

Mississippi while awaiting his six A.M. flight. His friend Mark Vaporis had offered to stay up with him, but Newell politely turned down his offer. "No, you need to get some sleep," Newell told him. "I don't think I will be able to sleep anyway." Newell spent the night sitting on a couch in the lobby of the dorm where the Habitat for Humanity volunteers were staying. He wanted to be alone in his thoughts and prayers. Twice during the night his silence was broken by sad, mournful phone calls from Carly. Newell found it difficult to comfort his daughter while hurting so much himself.

Early in the morning Mark fired up the bus the work crew took to the site every day and drove Newell to the airport. Even after he sat down on the crowded plane, Newell felt very much as if he were in a different world. *This just isn't possible . . . this just isn't possible,* he repeated to himself. He found solace in leaning his head against the window and crying and praying softly for his family. During his layover in Charlotte, Newell called his mother and the rest of his extended family to break the news to them. His plane arrived in Indianapolis shortly after noon.

Jim, Colleen, and the girls waited for Newell at the bottom of the escalator that led down to the baggage claim area of the airport. People came down the escalator in waves, not becoming fully visible until they were halfway down. As soon as Colleen caught a glimpse of Newell's legs, she knew it was him. She rushed toward the escalator and grabbed hold of him as soon as he stepped off. Carly, Sandra, and Laisa joined her. The people coming down the escalators gave them strange looks as they squeezed past. Finally the Ceraks pulled back from each other and headed toward Jim's car. Newell had left all his luggage with the construction team in Mississippi.

The Ceraks stopped at a Cracker Barrel between Indianapolis and Upland for lunch and to talk about what each of them had experienced the night before while they were apart. They knew they needed to eat, but they could hardly force the food into their emotionally spent bodies. The conversation around the table had a surreal quality to it. "Am I the only one who's having trouble coming to grips with this?" Newell asked at one point during the meal. "I just cannot believe she is gone."

"No," Carly said. "This feels like a bad dream and I wish I would wake up."

"Me too," Sandra said.

"Did they ask you to help identify Whitney's body last night?" Newell asked Carly.

"No. Someone else did that. Someone from the college, I think."

"I don't blame you. I don't think I want to see her body either. I don't want that image burned into my mind," Newell said.

"They asked me last night if I wanted to see her too, but I said no," Colleen said. "I would much rather remember her smiling at me, with those big dimples. That's the real Whitney, that's the Whitney that's in heaven right now. That's the picture I want to remember."

Newell picked at his food. He knew he should eat, but he no longer had an appetite. "This can't be happening," he said.

After arriving back at Taylor around three in the afternoon, the Ceraks faced the emotionally difficult task of cleaning out Whitney's things from her dorm room in Olson Hall. They opened the door on the south end of the hall only to find the lobby filled with all the residents, gathered to pray for those affected by the accident. The Ceraks could hear the head resident briefing the girls on the details of the accident, along with the girls' sobs. Quickly they closed the door, hoping no one noticed them. "I don't think I can walk into the middle of all those girls and answer all their questions," Carly said. Colleen and Newell agreed. They slipped in through the door that led through the laundry room and went directly to Whitney's room.

Emily, Whitney's roommate, and Amy and Anne, two of her friends who lived across the hall, left the prayer meeting and met the Ceraks in Whitney's room. The girls had already packed all her things to spare the family that trauma. "There's something I think Whitney would want you to have," Emily said. "A few weeks ago we started doing a Bible study together, just the four of us. Yesterday at the end of our Bible study Whitney made this and hung it over our door. She said she wanted this sign to be a reminder to serve God in everything she did. Anyway, I thought you would like to have it."

"Thank you," Newell said as he reached out and took the small sign. He turned it over and read it out loud. "Well done, good and faithful servant." His voice cracked, and he could barely get the words out. "Matthew 25:23. According to the Bible, these are the words with which Jesus will greet into heaven those who love Him." Tears began streaming down the faces of Colleen,

Carly, and Sandra. "Thank you," they said. "Thank you very much for giving this to us."

Jim Mathis volunteered to take Carly's friends back to Gaylord, which allowed the Ceraks time to be alone during their drive home. They went to Carly's room at the other end of Olson Hall so that she could pack whatever she needed for the trip home. And Whitney's funeral. Once they were in the car, Carly looked around and said, "I can't believe there are only three of us now." She began sobbing again. Newell could hardly start the car because of his tears. As he turned on the engine, a CD of praise and worship music began to play in the car stereo. Rather than turn it off, they allowed the music to wash over them. After a few miles the three of them began singing along with the songs of praise to God. It seemed only appropriate. However, as they passed the spot on the highway where truck tracks veered across the center median into the southbound lanes at mile marker 66, they stopped singing and began crying once again.

After an hour of music, Colleen turned the volume down low. "We need to plan what we are going to do when we get home. Tomorrow is Friday, and I would like to have Whit's funeral on Sunday. I want people to be able to come without having to take time off from work."

"Which means the viewing will be on her birthday," Newell said.

"That's okay," Colleen said. "In fact I think the timing fits. Whitney always loved birthday parties. It seems only right to have one last huge party to celebrate her life." Colleen completed her to-do list of all that would have to happen between Thursday afternoon and Sunday, and then turned to writing Whitney's obituary for the local paper.

About halfway through the trip, the sun sank low in the western sky. Newell looked out the window and said, "This is our first sunset without Whitney." The car fell silent for rest of the trip, except for the sound of gentle sobs from the backseat.

5

WAITING

"Wait for the Lord. Be strong and take heart,
and wait for the Lord." Psalm 27:14

Sunshine Girl, the waiting is the hardest. We know we have a mighty God. He is holding us up. He has you in His hands. He is sheltering you. God gave us a precious gift when He gave us you. You are a joy and we treasure you. We are asking God to restore you to full health and we know God loves us and you.

His ways are perfect.

Keep fighting, little one. Get stronger every day. Open your beautiful eyes. God's people are praying all over the world for you. So many that love you have been here. I hope you can hear our voices.

I love you—

Mom

NOTE FROM SUSIE VAN RYN TO LAURA
WHILE SHE WAS IN ICU, APRIL 27

Laura's neurologist from Parkview Hospital didn't pull any punches when she sat down with the family. "Laura is in a coma, and there are no guarantees that she will come out of it, or if she does, that she will be the same person she was before. You need to understand what we are dealing with here. Your daughter has a traumatic brain injury, caused by the violent force of the accident.

We do not yet know how extensive the damage may be, nor can I tell you what sort of recovery you may expect. So much is unknown. Only time will tell."

Don leaned forward in his chair. "How much time?" he asked.

"That could be anywhere from a matter of days to weeks to even longer."

Don turned to Susie, her face drained white. "I guess that means we won't be taking her back home in a couple of days, like we first thought," he said with a nervous laugh.

"No, your daughter will be here for a while. These injuries don't fit the Hollywood picture of a coma," the doctor went on to explain. "Your daughter is not just going to wake up one day like awakening from a long nap. Coming out of a coma is comparable to coming up from deep underwater. She will gradually come up closer to the surface over time. At this point we cannot say how close to the surface she will come, or if she will ever wake up completely."

Don nodded as he tried to process everything the doctor told them, his expression never changing. He appreciated the doctor's frank approach. *Okay,* he thought to himself, *at least now we know what we're dealing with.* "So what do we do next?" he asked.

"Our main concern right now is the swelling or bleeding in the brain," the doctor said. "We're going to keep an eye on it. We want the pressure to stay under twenty-five. Right now it is at sixteen, which is excellent. It may spike up over twenty from time to time, but don't get too alarmed. You need to know right from the start that Laura is going to have many, many ups and downs. Don't get too excited by a good sign, and don't get too down over a bad sign. We're going to have a lot of both by the time this is over."

Susie shifted in her seat. Outwardly, she struggled to remain calm for her children's sake. Inside, fear enveloped her. *If this doctor is trying to cheer us up, she isn't doing a very good job of it*, she thought. Rather than alleviate her fears and reassure her that everything would be all right, the doctor made Susie more anxious than ever. *Oh God*, she prayed, *whether Laura lives or dies is completely up to you. You know what I want, but I don't have any choice but to trust you and place my daughter in your care. Again.*

Don reached over and took her hand. "It's okay, Suz. We're not going through this alone." Then he asked the doctor, "Is there anything we can do to help?"

"Just your presence can help her, just being there. While we need to be careful not to overstimulate Laura, talking to her and letting her know you are there helps the neurons in her brain fire and reconnect. And of course, you can pray. I know you're already doing that."

"Lots of people are," Don replied.

Hey Laurie . . . We bought you this journal knowing how much you love to write. Some of the pages have been used, but hopefully there's some left for you. we love you, Laurie & miss seeing your smiley little face. Our prayers & thoughts are with you each day. You've touched so many lives & we know you are going to touch so many more. We wish you all the best and can't wait to give you a BIG, BIG hug! Love ya girl!

Love, Tegan, Liza, Pawdge

P.S. When you get better we are going to be singing Amy Grant "The Night Before Christmas" together @ church.

—Pawdge

Inscription on the first page of a journal (unedited) that Laura's friends placed in the ICU waiting room. Her friends and family wrote notes of encouragement for her to read when she awoke from her coma.

A crowd had already begun to form in the ICU lounge. A group of Laura's friends from Taylor talked on one side of the room, while Aryn sat over on the other with his parents. Aryn tried to avoid the crowds as much as possible. The family of another ICU patient sat in the cluster of chairs near the window. All the conversations stopped as the Van Ryns walked through the door. Aryn immediately got up and walked over to Don. "What did they say?" he asked.

Don took a deep breath. "The news could be better, but it could also be a lot worse." He went on to explain everything the neurologist had told them. As he and Aryn spoke, Paul and Sue Johnston, two close friends from Grand Rapids, came walking in. Susie went over and met them at the door. More friends and family soon followed, along with a steady stream of Taylor students. Lisa's, Kenny's, and Mark's friends arrived a short time later. By eleven A.M. the crowd was nearly standing room only, each of whom was greeted by a member of the Van Ryn family. Don looked around and said to Paul, "I almost feel like I'm hosting some big event here."

Due to the nature of her injuries, Laura's doctors severely limited both the number of visitors and the time they could spend in her room. Although her immediate family could see her whenever doctors or nurses were not in the middle of a procedure, other visitors were restricted to four half-hour visitation times spread throughout the day. And far more than immediate family came to the hospital every day.

By the time the first visitation period rolled around, the crowd hoping to see Laura spilled out of the ICU lounge and into the hall. "So, DV," Lisa said to Don (all four of the Van Ryn children called him DV rather than Dad), "how are we going to handle this?"

"I'm not sure. I guess we're going to have to make like tour guides and usher back those that want to see her a few at a time."

"We really have taken this place over," Lisa laughed. She looked back over at the crowd waiting. "You can do the dirty work."

"No problem," Don said. He turned and announced to the large group in the waiting room, "Hey, listen. The doctors will not allow any more than three or four people back with Laura at any one time. If you want to see her, we'll need you to line up and one of us will take you back. Now, keep in mind that you'll only have a few minutes. And please, keep it quiet. We need to keep the noise level to a minimum."

All over the waiting room, people stood and walked over to form a line in the hall. Don walked to the front of the line, counted off the first group of three, all of whom were close friends of Laura. He told them, "Lisa will take you back. We really appreciate you girls being here for Laura today. That means a lot to us."

Lisa led the girls back into the ICU area. A few minutes later, she brought them back out. None of the girls could speak when they first walked back into the hallway, tears streaming down their faces. They wrapped their arms around Lisa, then walked over to Susie and hugged her as well. "How is she?" someone asked. None of them could answer. Their words stuck in their throats.

Mark then led the next group back. Another followed. And another after that. And another after that. The scene repeated itself a few hours later during the next window in which visitors were allowed into the ICU area, and again and again over the next several days. None of the dozens' of visitors ever questioned the identity of the girl lying in the bed; or if they did, they never raised the question with the family or hospital staff. Throughout the time spent in intensive care, Laura's altered state and expressionless face *became* her identity. Despite her condition, Laura was exactly who they saw.

Some time between the first and second ICU visitation periods, Jay Curry dropped by. He'd never met Don or Susie before, but he had connected with Laura the night before. Jay walked over to Don and introduced himself. "I was one of the medics on the medi-flight helicopter that brought Laura in last night," he said. "How is she doing today?"

Don felt an immediate bond because this was one of the rescuers who'd saved his daughter's life. "She's alive thanks to you,"

Don said as he stood and embraced Jay. Then Jay sat down near the family, who started peppering him with questions.

"I know I'm not the only one to say this," Jay said, "but this was pretty much the worst accident scene I've ever come across. I hope I never see another one like it. Laura was the only one thrown from the vehicle who survived," he continued. "She was breathing on her own when we found her."

"That's really good news, right?" Lisa said to her mother and brothers.

"It is," Jay said. He went on to describe how quickly they had "packaged" Laura at the scene—that is, how they had stabilized her and prepared her for transit. "We had her here in twenty, maybe twenty-five minutes, after the call came in on the accident."

"Is that faster than normal?" Susie asked.

"For an accident like this, it sure is. The response time from all the rescue workers was really amazing," Jay said. "God was watching out for her," he added with a smile. "You could sense that at the accident scene. And I have to tell you, this one was pretty personal for me. I graduated from Taylor. Working on Laura was like working on family."

Not long after Jay left, another stranger walked in and began asking for the Van Ryn family. She came over to Don and Susie and said, "My name is Julie. You guys don't know me, but I felt like I had to come by to see you. When I heard about the accident last night on the news, the reporter said Laura was from Caledonia. My father-in-law owns a hardware store up there, so I know how far from home you are. I live here in Fort Wayne now, so if you need anything, please don't hesitate to ask."

"We really appreciate that," Don said, and he intended to leave it at that. Almost everyone who had been in to see them over the course of the previous twelve hours had said something close to the same thing.

"What are you doing for food while you are here?" Julie asked.

The family looked at one another and laughed. "So far it's been the hospital cafeteria and vending machines," Susie said.

"My husband and I own a Little Caesar's Pizza shop," Julie said. "Would you mind if we sent over some pizzas for you tonight?"

"We wouldn't mind at all, thank you so much," Lisa answered for the rest of them.

Don laughed. "Pizza does sound pretty good. That is very generous of you." He had no idea how generous Julie really was. Later that evening she and her young daughters walked in and stacked pizza boxes on the table in the ICU lounge. By the time they were finished, it looked like a pizza box skyscraper. Don estimated that there had to be at least twenty-five pizzas stacked up, of all different varieties. But none of it went to waste, not with a waiting room filled with college students. Don and Susie also shared the pizza with the families of other ICU patients who had camped out in the waiting room.

"Could you guys use some bottled water up here?" Julie asked when she delivered the pizzas. "I know buying water and sodas from the vending machines can get expensive."

"That would be wonderful. How can we ever thank you?" Susie said.

"You don't have to. And I hope you don't mind, but I called

my church and told them about your situation. It's called Pathway Community Church. Anyway, a lot of people from the church would like to bring you guys meals up here, if that's all right with you."

"I don't know what to say," Don said.

"How about yes?" Susie added.

Visitors streamed into the waiting room throughout the day. At around three in the afternoon Don needed a break from all the people. "I'm going to get some air," he told his family. He walked outside the hospital for the first time since they'd arrived early that morning. The sunshine felt good on his face. As he stood soaking it in, he stared out across the hospital parking lot. News crew vans with satellite relay antennas from both Fort Wayne and Indianapolis television stations had sprouted all around like mushrooms after a rain. The severity of the crash, along with the fact that the van was filled with college students and staff, made this a national story. A reporter walked over to Don and said, "Mr. Van Ryn? Would you mind if I asked you a couple of questions?"

How did this guy know it was me? Don wondered. "Sure. Go ahead," he said.

"We understand that the truck driver who caused this accident was also brought here last night. Have you talked to him?"

Wow. He was? "No," Don replied, "but I would like to." Don could see the reporter's eyes light up.

"And what would you like to say to him?" the reporter asked with an expression on his face that seemed to say, *Oh boy, here it comes!*

"I would like to tell him that I feel sorry for him and that I forgive him," Don said. The reporter's countenance seemed to drop. Apparently this wasn't the angry tirade he'd hoped for. "Harboring bitterness and anger isn't going to get you very far," Don continued. "God has shown me mercy and forgiven me. How can I help but do the same?"

After walking away, Don started thinking about the reporter's question and about Robert Spencer, the truck driver. No one yet knew why he'd crossed the center median and into the path of the Taylor van. The more Don thought about him, the more he imagined that this man must be dying inside. This hadn't been a malicious act. The driver hadn't set out to hurt anyone, and yet five people had died as a result of the accident. *I need to tell him how I feel,* Don thought.

He walked to the hospital front desk and asked the volunteer for Robert Spencer's room number. The desk attendant clicked away on the computer keys, then replied, "I'm sorry, but we have no record of a Robert Spencer being in the hospital."

"Are you sure?" he asked.

"Yes, sir."

"Hmmm. Okay. Thanks a lot," Don said and walked away. *That makes sense, the police protecting the driver like this. They probably aren't sure what this crazy dad might do if I found him. That's too bad. I really would like to tell him how we feel.*

When he returned to the ICU lounge, the waiting room phone rang. Someone answered the phone, then called out, "Is Don Van Ryn in here?"

"Yeah, right here," he answered as he walked over and took

the phone. "Who would call me on the hospital number?" he asked to no one in particular. All their friends and family that hadn't already driven to Fort Wayne would call his or Susie's cell phone, not the hospital number. He picked up the phone and said, "This is Don, may I help you?"

"Yes, Mr. Van Ryn, I represent a law firm in Washington, D.C., that specializes in truck and automobile accidents." The caller went on to give the firm's name and to describe their success in suing trucking companies and winning multimillion-dollar judgments for their clients.

Don was stunned. He could not believe he'd been tracked down at the hospital so soon after the accident. He'd always heard jokes about ambulance-chasing lawyers, but he never knew they really existed until this moment. "I'm not interested in talking to you, sir. I hope you can find something better to do with your day than this. Good-bye," Don said as he hung up the phone.

"Who was that?" Susie asked as Don sat down next to her.

"A lawyer. Can you believe that? Some ambulance-chasing attorney wanted to know if his firm could represent us in a lawsuit against the trucking company."

"Lawsuit? Are you serious? Of all the inappropriate times to ask such a question."

"Get ready. I have a feeling it won't be the last call like this that we get."

Late that afternoon one of the hospital chaplains approached Don and Susie. "Have you guys thought about where you're going to stay while you're here?"

"We haven't talked about it too much," Don said. "Honestly, we don't want to get too far away from right here."

"It would be nice to be able to take a shower, however," Susie added.

"I bet," the chaplain said. "That's why I came up here. Several years ago one of the pastors in town and his wife found themselves in the same situation you're in now. They had a child in an intensive care unit out of town, and they couldn't afford to stay in a hotel. That left them no place to stay except the waiting room. Once they got back here to Fort Wayne, they started soliciting donations from businesses and churches in the area to buy a house a couple of blocks from here. They named it Samaritan's House, and it's available for you and your family if you need it."

"Wow." Don paused. "Yes, we definitely need it. How much does it cost a night to stay there?"

"Nothing. Everything is taken care of. Bedding, toiletries, even food. Pastor Tom Foster—that's the name of the pastor who made this happen—wanted to make sure that families had everything they needed when they stayed there. If I had to guess, I would say you guys probably didn't exactly pack everything you needed for an extended stay down here, did you?"

"I think we have one toothbrush among the five of us," Susie said with a laugh.

"I think we can rustle up some for you," the chaplain said.

A little while later he took Don and Susie over to the house, where they were met by Pastor Tom. He showed them around and gave them a set of keys. Before Don and Susie walked back over to the hospital, Pastor Tom asked Don, "May I pray for you and your family?"

"You bet," Don replied. Don never forgot Tom's prayer for him there in the living room. Tom prayed that Don would be the father he needed to be for his family through this crisis.

A young Amish couple with a baby in the ICU were sleeping in one of the bedrooms the first few nights the Van Ryns stayed in the house. After they left, the family had the entire house to themselves. Aryn also stayed in the house and walked back and forth to the hospital. Don, Susie, and Lisa still didn't have the clothes or other personal essentials for a protracted stay far from home, but that soon changed as friends driving down from Grand Rapids offered to stop by their house and pick up whatever the family needed.

Life outside Parkview Hospital seemed to stand still. For Don and Susie and their children, caring for Laura was their single priority. From the start they knew they desperately needed as many people to pray for Laura as they could find. Little did they know that the way they would choose to inform those praying would arouse interest in Laura's story far beyond their circle of friends. Soon people around the world were checking in on Laura every day and lifting her up to God in prayer.

Thurs., April 27

This was a long day. You are loved by so many—I can't begin to name all the people who came by or called. Paul and Aunt Sue were here early. Also a real support to us. So many expressions of love, we have so much to be grateful for! I was shaky today, Laurie, wanting so badly for you to wake up. It's not like you to be so still! Your bruises and small cuts on your face look better even since we got here. We are meeting so many of God's people, His family is awesome. We are so blessed. Wake up, sweetie—I want to talk to you and see your beautiful face—look into your eyes. I love you, Mom.

From Susie's prayer journal

God, hear my prayers! I want to be so mad at your will, Lord, but I can't. You know how much I love her. Please, I pray, perform a miracle in her life. You are the great Healer. Do your thing ... I know that you will perform your will, and I pray that your will is a full recovery for her. You know I will always serve you no matter the situation. You know I would give my life for you. How I wish it was me in that bed instead of her, Father. She doesn't deserve this. It is so hard to just sit around all day. Please give me peace knowing that you are at work. Life is so short, Lord, what a reminder this is ... Please sustain us ... I love you, Lord—Your faithful servant.

ARYN'S PRAYER FOR LAURA, APRIL 28, 2006

6

COMFORT IN THE
MIDST OF PAIN

WHITNEY ERIN CERAK, age 18 of Gaylord, Michigan, died in a tragic car accident Wednesday, April 26, 2006, in Marion, Indiana. She was born in Muncie, Indiana, on April 29, 1987, to Newell and Colleen Cerak. She lived a wonderful and full but short life. She attended Gaylord Community Schools from kindergarten to twelfth grade, where she made many friends and endeared herself to all. She was very active in sports, student government, and the E-Free Youth Group. She was a freshman at Taylor University, where she was growing in love and knowledge of her Friend and Savior, Jesus Christ. She is now living with Him in heaven. She is survived by her parents, Newell and Colleen Cerak; sister Carly; "sister" Sandra; and many relatives. Funeral services for Whitney will be held on Sunday, April 30, at 3 P.M. at Gaylord Evangelical Free Church. Visitation will be on Saturday at the Nelson Funeral Home from 3 to 8 P.M. and on Sunday at the church from 2 P.M. until the time of services. Memorial contributions may be made to the Invisible Children through the Nelson Funeral Home.

WHITNEY'S OBITUARY FROM THE *GAYLORD HERALD TIMES* ON
MAY 2, 2006. NEWELL, COLLEEN, AND CARLY WROTE IT WHILE
DRIVING HOME FROM TAYLOR THE DAY AFTER THE ACCIDENT.

Colleen couldn't believe it as she walked through her back door into the kitchen. "This doesn't look like our house," said to Newell and Carly. They had come into the house through the back breezeway, where they found the bench next to the door covered with cases of water and coolers of Pepsi. Newell opened a refrigerator someone had dropped off while they were gone. "Look at this, Colleen. It's stuffed with food."

But it was the kitchen that blew them both away. Six huge bouquets of flowers ringed the counter, and what space wasn't covered by floral arrangements held large trays of cookies. The food spilled out into the dining room, and flowers covered every flat space throughout the downstairs. Colleen touched her hand to her mouth and fought back tears. Newell and Carly walked over to her, and the three wrapped their arms around one another.

After a few minutes Carly walked over to the telephone answering machine that sat on a small shelf in the space between the kitchen and dining room. "I wonder if the machine is broken," she said. "The lights are flashing, but there's not a number on it like there usually is."

"That's odd," Newell said. He pressed the play button. A mechanical female voice said, "You have thirty-one messages. Message one . . ." For the next fifteen minutes the three of them sat in the kitchen and listened as the answering machine played thirty-one variations of the same message: "Hi, Colleen and Newell. This is . . . I just heard about the accident. I can't believe it. I am so, so sorry. I love you guys so much and I'm praying for you, and for Carly and Sandra too. If you need anything, please let me know." The three of them were silent as the messages played. They simply sat and soaked in the expressions of love and concern.

Then Colleen pulled a pen and paper out of a drawer and replayed the tape, writing down the names of everyone who had called.

Newell, Colleen, and Carly walked through the house, reading the cards on the flower arrangements along with the other notes and cards. Sandra joined them when a friend dropped her off. They could not believe so many people had done so much so quickly. Colleen had left the house for Upland barely twenty-four hours earlier. Yet at the same time, each of them struggled to accept that this was happening to *them*. They felt pulled between two poles. One of gratitude for all the expressions of love, the other of grief over Whitney's death. "She touched so many lives," Colleen said, her voice breaking. "So many lives in such a short time."

Admiring the flowers and reading the cards and notes took the family from the kitchen, through the dining room, into the living room, to the staircase. Newell looked back at Colleen and the girls. "We need to go up now," he said. They knew what he meant. The four of them slowly climbed the stairs and walked into Whitney's bedroom. The bed was made and everything was in its place, which was not the norm when Whitney lived at home. But since she had moved away to college, her room stayed neat and clean, at least until she came home. "I guess her room will always be clean now," Newell said. He meant it as a joke, and they all laughed. Quickly the laughter turned into tears.

The four of them lay down on Whitney's bed and held one another. No one said anything for a very long time. All felt an overpowering sense of emptiness. Eventually Carly broke the silence. "I remember one time Whitney and I . . ." That broke the ice for the family. As they lay on Whitney's bed mourning her death, they began sharing stories that brought her life into the room. Most of the stories left them laughing. They talked about Whitney's infectious smile and her mischievous sense of humor. Nothing would ever take away those memories, but the realization that memories were all they had left made them break down in tears again.

"I really don't know how life can go on without her," Newell said. "I can't believe she's not going to burst through that door right now and ask us what we're all crying for."

"Yeah, she'd probably accuse me of coming in to steal her clothes," Carly said, Everyone laughed, and then the room fell silent.

After what seemed like a long time, Colleen said, "I don't know how we're going to do the holidays this year. I can't imagine making Christmas cookies without her helping. Or decorating the tree. Or Christmas morning without her busting down the stairs."

"Or watching *White Christmas*," Carly said. They'd watched the old Bing Crosby and Danny Kaye classic every year since Carly and Whitney were little girls. The two of them could sing every song. They would dance around the living room singing "Sisters," which they especially loved. Carly had to stop even thinking about it.

"You know," Newell said, "every Memorial Day Whit would watch *Saving Private Ryan* with me. It's such a violent movie, and not exactly the kind of film she'd usually watch. But she insisted on watching it with me on Memorial Day. I asked her why once.

She told me she wanted to remember why we're celebrating Memorial Day. Said she didn't want to forget why those people died for us." He paused, tears streaming down his face. "That's just a couple of weeks away . . ." His voice trailed away and he couldn't finish his thought.

"I'll watch it with you, Dad," Carly said. The two of them cried even harder. The realization of what life would be like without Whitney was beginning to set in.

Their long to-do list awaited Colleen and Newell when they woke up around eight-thirty on Friday morning. Although holding Whitney's viewing on Saturday and her funeral on Sunday seemed like a good idea while driving home from Upland, much had to be done to make these events happen. They had not yet talked with the funeral home to coordinate services that would begin in just under thirty hours. Colleen and Newell also needed to pick out a casket, buy a burial plot, and make all the other arrangements for the funeral. On top of that, the Grant County coroner's office had not yet released Whitney's body. That meant more phone calls to make sure it would arrive in Gaylord in time for all they had planned.

All of these things swirled in Colleen's head as she climbed out of bed and went downstairs to get started. Carly met her in the living room. "You know what, Mom? I think we need to spend two hours in prayer before we try to face today."

Colleen looked at her with a look of utter disbelief. *Two hours!* she thought. *Don't you know what we have to do today? We don't have two hours to spare.* "That's a nice idea, Carly," she said, "but I have too much to do. I don't know how I will ever get it all done."

"Mom, this isn't a request," Carly replied. "We have to do this. If we don't start off our day getting our strength from God, we won't survive this." Colleen tried to respond, but Carly wouldn't hear it. She'd already started toward the front door with a sign in her hand that read "Please do not disturb us until eleven."

After a light breakfast, Carly turned off the phones and gathered her mother and father and Sandra into the living room. Each one brought a Bible. Colleen couldn't concentrate on anything but the list of things she absolutely had to get done as soon as possible. Perhaps sensing the thoughts running through her mother's head, Carly said, "Before we do anything else, I want to play a couple of worship songs just to get our minds off what we need to do today, and put them on the Lord." She then pressed "play" on the CD player.

> *I was sure by now that You would have reached down*
> *   and wiped our tears away*
> *Stepped in and saved the day*
> *But once again, I say "Amen," and it's still raining*
> *As the thunder rolls I barely hear You whisper through*
> *   the rain, "I'm with you"*
> *And as Your mercy falls I raise my hands and praise the*
> *   God that gives and takes away*
> *I'll praise You in this storm, and I will lift my hands*
> *For You are who You are, no matter where I am*

*Every tear I've cried You hold in your hand, You never
left my side
And though my heart is torn, I will praise You in this
storm.* *

The song lyrics felt as if they'd been penned specifically for the family in this very moment. Tears flowed. In a matter of seconds God's
presence enveloped them, causing Colleen and everyone else in
the room to forget all about funeral arrangements and phone calls.

Carly played another song or two, then asked her dad to lead
the family in prayer. After the prayer, she took out the Bible that
Whitney had received as a high school graduation present less
than a year earlier. A few weeks before the accident, Whitney and
a few friends from her wing in Olson Hall had started studying
the book of Psalms together. Whitney had never written in her
Bible before, but during this study, she began underlining verses
God used to speak to her: "He lifted me out of the slimy pit, out
of the mud and mire, he set my feet on a rock and gave me a firm
place to stand" (Psalm 40:2) . . . "Because your love is better than
life, my lips will glorify you" (Psalm 63:3) . . . "Find rest, O my
soul, in God alone; my hope comes from him . . . Trust in him at
all times, O people; pour out your heart to him, for God is our
refuge" (Psalms 62:5 and 8).

As Carly began reading these passages that had meant so much
to Whit, the Ceraks felt as if Whitney were right there with them.

---

*"Praise You in this Storm," by Mark Hall. EMI CMG Publishing Copyright
2005, International Copyright Secured. All Rights Reserved. Used by Permission.

"To me," Carly said, "this verse sounds like Whitney is telling us what she's seeing and hearing right now. 'How lovely is your dwelling place, O Lord Almighty! My soul yearns, even faints, for the courts of the Lord; my heart and flesh cry out for the living God' (Psalm 84:1–2)."

Everyone fell silent for several minutes. Finally Newell said, "Second Corinthians 1:3 and 4 calls God the 'Father of compassion and the God of all comfort, who comforts us in all our troubles.' I don't think I ever really understood what it was talking about until right now." His voice broke and tears began running down his face. "I know the accident that took Whitney's life did not take God by surprise. I don't know how I can go on without her, but I know He didn't leave us alone to try to figure this out on our own." He stopped and tried to hold himself together. "Thanks, Carly, for making us stop and focus on God rather than everything we have to do. I'm glad you wouldn't take no for an answer."

The time of prayer and worship flew by. At ten-thirty Jim Mathis stuck his head in the door and said, "I'm sorry to disturb you, but I needed to tell you that I set up an appointment for you at Nelson's funeral home at eleven-thirty A.M." As quickly as he had popped in, he disappeared. No one else knocked on the door or bothered the family in any way. Then at the stroke of eleven, their calm sanctuary turned into Grand Central Station. The moment the family turned off the music, raised the shades, and turned the phones back on, a whirlwind of activity set in. Friends from the church where Newell had served as a youth pastor for eighteen years came by, as did delivery people from the local florists.

Newell, Colleen, Carly, and Sandra soon left for the funeral home, where they met with Carol Nelson, whom they'd known since moving to Gaylord. "Do you have any idea about what kind of casket you would like?" she asked.

"Don't take this the wrong way," Colleen said, "but we don't want to spend much money. Whitney's in heaven, she's not here."

"I understand," Carol said. "I understand completely." Then she added, "I'm so sorry you have to go through this," as she fought back tears. She then led Newell, Colleen, Carly, and Sandra down into the basement room, where all the caskets were on display. "I'll leave you down here to make a decision on your own. Don't hesitate to ask if you have any questions. Take as much time as you need."

After Carol went back upstairs, Newell said to Colleen, "It feels like this is happening to someone else. I almost feel like I'm outside my body watching all this."

"I know," Colleen said.

"It hurt when my dad died, but children are supposed to bury their parents. Parents aren't supposed to plan their daughter's funeral. It seems like you just took her shopping for a prom dress; now we're picking out a casket."

"I can't quite wrap my mind around that one, either. So what do you think? Which one should we get?" Colleen asked.

"If it were up to Whit, she'd say get a pine box and send the money we would spend on a nice casket to the Invisible Children."

"I don't see any pine boxes, but this one over here looks nice,

69

and it's the next to the cheapest one they have. She'd probably say to get this one."

"I like it too," Newell said.

When the Ceraks returned to their house, it was anything but quiet. A constant parade of friends and family came through the door. Colleen's friends took over the kitchen, while others kept track of everyone who had come by. Whitney and Carly's friends also began streaming in.

The day flew by, yet it never lost its unreal feeling. Carly and Sandra were in and out of the house. By late afternoon Colleen found Newell and said, "Let's get out of here for a little bit."

"What do you have in mind?" he asked.

"I know this is going to sound crazy, but the high school girls have a home soccer game today. I think we should go," she said. The idea didn't sound crazy to Newell. Whitney had been one of the team's captains the previous season and all the girls on the current team, with the exception of the freshmen, had been her teammates. The fact that they could even bring themselves to play a game two days after her death was remarkable.

The match was already well under way when Newell and Colleen walked up to the field. They didn't want to be around a lot of people, nor did they want to take away from the girls on the field by having to answer everyone's questions, so they stood by the fence alongside the field, far from their usual place the previous season. Even from there they could see that each girl on the team had wrapped a piece of white athletic tape around the top of her socks. On the tape was written, "Whit #9," along with a personal message for Whitney. As soon as the match was over, the entire team, touched that the Ceraks would leave their house and come to their game at a time like this, flocked around Newell and Colleen and presented them with the messages they'd written for Whitney.

The rest of Friday flew by. Colleen dove into finalizing the arrangements for the next day's visitation. She asked a friend to put together a video presentation to play at Whitney's funeral. Colleen and Newell worked frantically for the next hour, sorting through pictures and videotapes for him. All the while, they continued to play host to the people streaming into the house.

At the end of the day, the two stumbled into bed exhausted. They fell asleep listening to the sound of music rising up from their basement. Carly and Sandra had gathered all their friends, along with Whitney's friends from high school and college. All these young people sang songs of praise to God and shared memories of Whitney. It seemed the only appropriate way to end the day.

7

FROM FORT WAYNE TO SYDNEY AND EVERY POINT IN BETWEEN

Friday, April 28, 2006
Friday update: This is an update on Laura's condition as of Friday morning...

INITIAL BLOG ENTRY

It started with an email. On the second day of waiting at Parkview Hospital, Todd Henderson sat down next to Lisa and said, "Did you know the hospital has free Wi-Fi right here in the waiting room?"

Lisa didn't know where Todd planned to go with this conversation. "Uh, okay. So that means you can check the Tigers' score if you want?"

"That's not exactly what I had in mind. If you'd like, I can send out an email update so that you and your family won't have to make so many phone calls every day."

"That would be awesome. It gets pretty old repeating the same news over and over on the phone."

"Just let me know what you want to say. In fact, if you want, you can use my computer and send it out through your own email account."

"That would probably work better," Lisa said. "That way people won't think this is spam coming from someone they don't know." She wrote an update, and then she and Todd spent the next hour putting together a list of names and email addresses that included family and friends from church, Taylor, and Upper Peninsula Bible Camp, where the Van Ryns worked every summer.

Many of those who received the email forwarded it to people they knew would faithfully pray for Laura. They in turn forwarded it to still more people. As the email spread, Lisa's inbox quickly filled up with responses from those who were praying and from those who wanted the latest on Laura's condition.

The next day Dave Niffin, a family friend who'd come to the hospital, watched Lisa trying to update her email list. "I never imagined so many people would want a daily update," Lisa said.

"Have you ever thought about doing a blog?" Dave asked.

"I wouldn't even know where to start."

"It's really easy to do, and a lot less work for you. People can still reply by leaving comments, which makes it more like a conversation."

Lisa talked it over with her family, and they agreed that it sounded like a good idea. It sure beat making a lot of phone calls every day, and then worrying that they might leave someone out.

Dave created an account for Lisa at blogspot.com and showed her how to log on and how to post entries. On Friday, April 28, two days after the accident, she put her first post on the Laura Van Ryn blog:

Laura is in Parkview Hospital in Fort Wayne, Indiana. She was air-lifted here Wednesday night. The accident occurred when Laura and her coworkers were traveling back to campus after setting up a banquet for Taylor, Fort Wayne. A semi-truck crossed the median on I-69 and hit the 15-passenger van Laura was traveling in. It hit toward the back of the left side of the van and ripped it open. Laura was thrown about 50 feet from the van and seemed to take the brunt of the force on her left side. Laura is currently in a co-matose state, and has been unconscious since the accident. This morning she made some small movements. There was a small move of her leg, squinting of the eyes, and some small finger movements . . . It is apparent she feels pain, which is actually a good sign. It also appears that she has been making some small self-generated movements. The family is extremely grateful for all the love that has been shown.

The next day she wrote:

Laura started moving a lot more throughout the day Friday, and her movement continues today. At times she squeezes hands, wig-gles toes, squints her eyes (though still closed), and moves her legs and arms. She is still in a comatose state, but her movements are a very positive sign. The doctors are emphasizing that it will be a "marathon and not a sprint," so improvements may be slow. Your prayers have been felt and God's hand has been upon Laura.

Please continue to pray for Laura, for the families who have lost children, and for all those who will be traveling to the funerals.

On Sunday she posted:

Yesterday [Laura] developed a fever of about 102.5. The cause was unknown, but this morning the fever has come back down. The most positive sign is the fact that she appeared to be responding to commands from the nurse this morning. Before this point, she had been moving and there were a lot of questions if the movements were voluntary or involuntary. It appears that this morning's movements were voluntary, which is obviously a very positive sign … A concern they have right now is pneumonia. Apparently, if someone is on a respirator for at least five days it is almost a natural occurrence for them to develop pneumonia. Monday night will be five days. Please continue to pray for Laura and the family, especially for these issues that require God's healing.

On Monday afternoon she added,

[Laura] had a good night Sunday, with stable vitals, no fever, no swelling of the brain. Her lungs are okay and there isn't any sign of pneumonia. Her nurse told her to put her thumbs up if she understood her, and Laura raised her thumbs! Keep in mind, she is still in a comatose state, but she is sporadically responding to commands/ requests now.

All of the early posts followed the same pattern: "Here are the facts . . . keep praying." Then one week after starting the blog, Lisa wrote,

> Laura is doing well this morning, and we continue to cling to the Lord's promises. From Psalm 33:20–22: "We wait in hope for the Lord; he is our help and our shield. In him our hearts rejoice, for we trust in his holy name. May your unfailing love rest upon us, O Lord, even as we put our hope in you." Here's an update for you all this morning . . .

From that day forward, the blog ceased to be merely an update on Laura's medical condition. The family wanted to do more than let people know Laura had survived; they wanted all who logged onto the blog to know that God remains faithful even when our worst nightmares become reality.

As the blog caught on, the phone calls and emails slowed down, as the family had hoped would happen. The blog contained a place for readers to post comments. To the family's surprise and encouragement, comments started coming in almost immediately. At first there were only a few a day, mostly from friends and family.

> I have been so fortunate to have all of you be such a vital and constant influence in my life. My soul rejoices at each post of good news. Our challenged and minuscule minds are such that we cannot understand what God's got brewin' up there. The only

thing that I do understand is that he does have something planned for this that may never be evident while we reside here on this earth. Everyone back at home has Laura and everyone close to her constantly in their prayers and thoughts. I love you all so very much from the bottom of my heart.

Bry.

Soon, word of the blog spread beyond Michigan and Indiana. The Van Ryns knew the Taylor community was strong, but as word of the blog passed from Taylor family to Taylor family, they learned how strong the ties within the community really were. One morning they logged on and found:

We have been praying for the Taylor community, the families of those who have "graduated" to heaven and for Laura's full recovery. We are missionaries in Germany and have kept updated through our son, a junior at Taylor, the TU website, and your blog. We have asked friends of ours to pray as well. We know that you take great comfort in knowing that Laura is in the hands of the Great Physician. We are praying for the staff at the hospital as they care for her and for strength and endurance for you as a family during this "marathon" (hopefully mini marathon). Most of all we are praying that through all of this people will be drawn to Christ as they read your messages and watch your lives. We are praying that you will sense His presence and grace in your life as you never have before and that Laura will wake up sooner than anyone ever expects!

Word of the blog even went beyond people who were re-motely connected to the Van Ryn family. A comment from someone in Arizona told them how a local Christian radio station gave regular updates on Laura's condition and asked its listeners to pray for her. One morning, the Van Ryns received this short note:

> May God bless you and keep you, may He make His face shine upon you … Even all the way over here in the Philippines, some are praying.

Dave Niffin, who had set up the blog, told the family that in the first two weeks of its existence, visitors had logged on from every corner of the United States and Canada, as well as from China, the Philippines, Colombia, Germany, Australia, Japan, and Africa. On May 10 alone, over 1,500 different people logged on, which was up from 1,300 the day before.

Not only did people from around the world closely monitor Laura's progress, they began expressing a real connection with her.

> Dear Van Ryn Family:
>
> Just want you to know that I'm praying for your family and that Laura will wake up. Thank you so much for setting up this blog and for sharing details—her pigtails, sitting in a chair, etc. It's great to picture what Laura is doing!

Others expressed sentiments that showed the reader wasn't just following Laura's condition out of curiosity. They thought of her throughout the day.

Today God gave me this verse and I believe it is for you too: "He who goes out with weeping carrying seed to sow, will return with songs of joy, carrying sheaves with him." I believe that through this time of struggle, there is a great plan for Laura and for all of you. I pray that you are encouraged each day by Laura's progress and the love of all of your friends and family. Laura, I love you!! Praying for you all the time.

    Connie

Following Laura's progress became some people's daily routine. As one commenter wrote:

Like most people who commented today, I check Laura's blog daily. And I have never met any of you. I graduated from Taylor nine years ago but that connection with the Taylor family is a strong one. So I feel like I'm still there, a part of all the grieving. You will continue to be in my prayers daily. Thanks for the updates.

The family read the comments every day as a source of encouragement. However, the comments showed that this dynamic was truly reciprocal. As one wrote:

Reading about Laura is one of the most encouraging parts of my day. Her/your family's story is such a cool testimony of God's work in the details of our lives. It's so encouraging to remember that God cares about things like ChapStick and pink balloons. So often I don't take the time to thank Him for all of the little blessings I receive every day. Thanks for helping me to open my eyes to the small things God does ... often the smallest things are truly the biggest.

But of all the people who kept close tabs on Laura's condition through the blog, none meant more to the Van Ryns than the family members of the other accident victims. Lisa could hardly contain her emotions when she logged on one day and read:

Hello, I am Monica Felver's oldest daughter. I wanted you and your family to know that you all are in my thoughts and prayers every day. I feel that we all have a connection, a bond due to the events that occurred on 4-26-06. I check Laura's progress daily and I am so grateful to hear her progress. As I am currently struggling to make it through the day, I am finding comfort in Jesus Christ our Lord and Savior. He is an amazing God and I have felt that he has smiled on each of our lives. Thank you for your wonderfully encouraging updates every day. Give Laura a hug from me. Take care, and may God bless you and your family. Love in him,

Kelly

Soon they received comment from Brad Larson's sister. She wrote:

Hi Van Ryns. What a blessing you are to so many people. I was honored to spend time with you on Friday, I hope that it is not long before I see you all again. I shared this verse with Lisa on Friday, but I love it so much. Zephaniah 3:17: "The Lord your God is with you, he is mighty to save. He will take delight in you, he will quiet you with his love, he will rejoice over you with singing." The Lord is definitely rejoicing over your family right now for your faithfulness to Him during this time. I love all of you daily and haven't stopped praying for you.

Dawn

Then, on May 11, they found this comment on the blog:

Thank you for the updates … please know that we are praying for Laura and for you. Our hearts go out to you in these very anxious and sleepless days. May God continue to strengthen you.

Newell and Colleen Cerak

By the time Lisa stopped writing the blog five weeks later, the daily comments numbered in the hundreds and came largely from complete strangers. Each day the Van Ryns read through all the comments. Every note of encouragement caused them to feel as though God Himself had walked into the waiting room and wrapped His arms around them. They needed it, for their journey was only getting started.

8

FIRST MILESTONE

Monday, May 1, 2006

Tomorrow morning, Laura is scheduled to go into surgery at 8:30. The fact that they are planning on doing surgery at this point is good news; it means they believe she is stable enough to handle a number of procedures. First, they will be setting her broken elbow and leg (femur) and possibly inserting pins where necessary. After the accident, they set them temporarily and now they will be setting them for good. While Laura is under, they will also do a tracheotomy. This has a number of purposes. They will remove the ventilator from her mouth and throat and insert it directly into the trachea at the incision point. This will help to reduce the risk of infection from the ventilator. This will also reduce the risk for pneumonia and lessen the severity of pneumonia, if she was to get it. The tracheotomy will also increase the potential to take Laura off the ventilator sooner.

When they do the surgery tomorrow, they will probably remove the tube from her head that monitors her intercranial pressure (ICP). This is the device that has been measuring any potential swelling of the brain. Since they haven't detected any significant swelling and pressure, they expect to remove it.

Please continue to pray and pass this along to your prayer groups.

BLOG ENTRY POSTED BY LISA VAN RYN

"Laura has improved nicely over the past few days. We've been very encouraged by her progress. However..." The moment

Laura's doctor said the word *however*, Susie felt as if her heart had stopped. She had to remind herself to breathe. "However, we need to do a number of procedures for her to recover fully. We would like to do these tomorrow morning."

"What exactly do you have in mind, doctor?" Don asked.

"Having her on the ventilator is helping her body recover from the trauma of this accident, but it also presents some risks. We would like to do a tracheotomy, which will allow us to remove the ventilator from her mouth and insert it directly into the trachea. This should reduce the risk of infection and also decrease Laura's risk of developing pneumonia. We also need to set her broken elbow and stabilize her broken legs. That means putting in some pins and possibly a plate. Right after the accident we set these temporarily, but now we would like to fix them permanently."

"She'll have a lot of fun going through metal detectors at the airport after this," Lisa joked. No one minded the touch of humor. If anything, they needed it.

"How long will the surgery take?" Susie asked.

"Not too long," the doctor said. "If you have no objections, we will schedule it for eight-thirty tomorrow morning and get her all fixed up."

Don and Susie signed off the needed paperwork, then leaned back and looked at each other. "Well, that's good news, right?" Don said. "She's strong enough to handle the surgery, which means it shouldn't be too long before she's strong enough to get out of ICU and move into a regular room."

Susie bristled at the thought. While the news that Laura had been in the accident had been hard to deal with, she had adjusted to the routine of the ICU. The lights and sounds of the machines still bothered Susie, but she knew what to expect when she walked into Laura's room. She did not like the idea of something new being sprung on her now.

"It's going to be all right, Mom. You'll see," Lisa said as she took her mother's hand. "God's in control."

"I know He is," Susie said. "I know." she let out a sigh. "Otherwise you'd probably have to find a room here for me as well."

"You're going to have an operation tomorrow," Susie said as she stroked Laura's hair. "The doctor said this should make your arm and leg feel a lot better." Aryn sat on the other side of the bed, holding Laura's hand. But for the lights on the monitors, the room was nearly dark. The heart monitor machine let out an odd sound, then immediately went back to a normal rhythm. Neither Susie nor Aryn flinched as they had on Laura's first day in the hospital. By this point they had grown accustomed to the sights and sounds of the ICU.

Susie didn't know if Laura could hear or understand her, but it didn't matter. She continued stroking her daughter's hair and said, "People all over the world are praying for you, sunshine girl. You can't believe how much you are loved." She leaned down and lightly kissed Laura's forehead. "You're going to come through this surgery just fine."

"We probably need to let her rest," Don said as he and the rest of the family walked into Laura's room. No sooner were the words out of his mouth than Laura let out a long yawn. The ventilator tube obscured their view, but they could all clearly see that she'd yawned, her first since the accident. Her eyelids then fluttered, and she opened her eyes just a bit.

"Did you see that?!" Susie exclaimed. "It looks like she's trying to wake up!" The rest of the family hugged and gave one another high fives. A yawn and a flutter of the eyelids may not seem like much, but after five days of very little response at all, it was huge.

"I'd say that's the perfect way to end the day," Don said.

"You and Suz can go get some sleep," Lisa said. "Mark and I will stay later tonight."

"I don't want to leave her," Susie said.

"It's okay, Mom, we'll be here. Besides, tomorrow's going to be a lot harder day on you than on Laura. You need to get some rest." After a little more convincing, Susie finally agreed. Everyone left the room and went back to Samaritan's House, except for Lisa and Mark. As they always did when they sat with their sister, the two of them stayed close to her bed and just watched her. A short while later Laura let out another big yawn. "Huh?" Lisa said.

"What?" Mark said.

"Her teeth."

"What about them?"

"They don't look right." The two of them leaned in for a closer look. It took a couple of minutes, but Laura finally yawned again. "Did you see it?" Lisa said.

Mark pointed to his incisors. "Those two right there are pushed up. That's really weird," he said.

"I know they said she'd been thrown over fifty feet. Wow. Can you imagine an impact strong enough to jam her teeth up like that? It's a miracle she survived the accident at all."

"Other than that, she looks pretty much normal, don't you think?" Mark said. "The swelling in her face is gone."

"But she won't like that shaved spot on her head from the spike," Lisa joked.

Although Laura's surgery was scheduled for 8:30 A.M., she wasn't taken to be prepped for surgery until well after noon. One of the surgeons had an emergency that pushed Laura's time back. Once again, the family found themselves waiting and waiting and waiting while they experienced firsthand the one hard and fast rule of waiting rooms: Surgeries always start later and last longer than you expect.

When the doctor finally came out of the operating room at 4:15 P.M., he gave the family a reassuring smile. "Everything went very well. Laura did great. We didn't have any complications of any kind. It all went exactly like we had hoped." The family let out a collective sigh of relief. Mark and Kenny gave each other a high five, while Lisa hugged her mother. "You will be able to see her soon, but she won't be as responsive as yesterday. She is still very sedated from the surgery."

"Were you able to do everything you'd talked about earlier?" Don asked.

"Yes. Like I said, the whole thing came off without a hitch.

Also, we should be able to remove the spike a little later today. We can do that in her room."

Just under an hour later, a nurse walked into the waiting room and said, "A couple of you can go back to see her now."

As Don and Susie walked into their daughter's room, they immediately noticed a change. "Her color looks so much better," Susie said, smiling. With the ventilator attached to the tracheal tube, nurses were now able to effectively remove any excess fluid from Laura's lungs, which improved her respiration. "Ahh, and she looks so much better with that horrible tube and tape off her beautiful mouth." Susie leaned down and gave her daughter a light kiss on her cheek.

Laura sported new casts on her left arm and leg. Her right arm was in a sling and had been tied down to keep her from grabbing at her tubes. The cuts on her face were healing nicely; however, she still did not show any expression whatsoever. The heart monitor beeped at a slower rate than it had a few days earlier. Her heart rate, which had been as high as 125, was now in the 80s. Laura remained very still the rest of Tuesday and most of Wednesday.

Don walked into the waiting room and noticed Lisa had her laptop open, working on her blog entry for the day. "Hey, Lis," he said, "would you be sure to ask people to pray that she comes out of this coma soon? We've had so many positive signs with all of her other injuries. We need people to pray that God wakes her up soon. And while you are at it, would you also ask them to pray for her emotional well-being after she wakes up? She's going to have a lot of tragic news to sort through. I don't know how we're going to break it all to her."

"Yeah, sure, DV," Lisa said. Then she typed, "Don's request today is that you pray for her to come out of the coma soon . . ."

People say we are so strong. Don't believe it! You know what a wimp I am! Being lifted up in prayer is my only explanation. My fears are many for you "little one," but God is greater than my fears. Sleep well, sweet Laurie. I love you so much — Mom.

Susie's note to Laura from Tuesday, May 2

9

"HAPPY BIRTHDAY, WHITNEY"

Dearest Whit,

Happy 19th Birthday!!! I'm so excited for you because you had the best birthday ever! I hope you didn't eat too many funfetti cup-cakes. The birthday fairy missed you this year, but he knows God took care of it. Lucky for you, the party never stops.

So, Whit, it's been way too long since we've talked. I *really* miss our Thursday night talks. I don't know if I ever told you, but I really looked forward to those. It's funny cuz only a week would go by and we could still talk about stuff for hours. That's just you, though—real easy to talk to. I'm not sure how I'm going to fill that time slot, but just know that I'm so grateful that our friendship wasn't damp-ered [*sic*], even though we went to different schools.

I have to tell you something that I never told you. I admire you. I admire you because you have to be the *only* girl I know who hates shopping. My mom wishes that some of that about you would rub off on me, so I'm going to work on that. I also admire you because you had such a heart for people. You made a point to make people feel loved, and I really saw that when everything with Liz happened. Oh, how I am so happy that you're with her now. Hug her for me. Whit, you're an amazing listener. There are few people who can work in a nursing home and be good at it. You would have been *amazing* at it because of your passion for it was so real. But Whit, above all, I admire your faith. I remember in high school you would always say you looked up to me and viewed me as strong. But the truth is ... you were *my* role model. I have my faith because of you. You got me involved and I've just come such a long way. It's really neat to hear how you've grown this year. I'm so thankful you went to Taylor and succeeded at getting that desire for God that you prayed about. He's so good.

Whit, I'm so grateful that God blessed me with you. I think you were my angel in disguise who was sent to get me through some of the hardest times in my life. You'll continue to be there, I know. Thanks.

All right, Whit ... I'm not going to lie ... I miss you a *ton*. It's going to be really hard when the people are gone, when we have dinner, holidays, when college graduation happens, when Car and I get married and later have kids. Just so you know—I'd never eat pretzel salad again if I could hug you one last time. Sometimes I wonder how I'm going to make it without you. But then I know ... God gives me peace, He gives me strength, and when I feel the weakest, He'll pick me up and carry me. Thanks Whit for showing me that. I love you with my *whole* heart and I know you're always here. So yeah, I love you and it's not good-bye—it's I'll see you later.

Love always,
the girl who lives in your basement
also known as your sister

LETTER SANDRA WROTE WHITNEY, SATURDAY, APRIL 29, 2006.
SHE READ THE LETTER AT WHITNEY'S FUNERAL THE NEXT DAY.

Colleen began crying softly as she awakened. "I've known since the day we dropped her off at Taylor that today would be different, but ... but not like this."

Newell pulled her close. "I know." He didn't say anything more. His mind drifted to Whitney's previous eighteen birthdays. He could picture her running into the kitchen, a big smile on her face, as he cooked her favorite breakfast, scrambled eggs with cheese and sausage.

"The timing of all of this . . . ," Colleen said. "It's just so . . ."

"Wrong," Newell said.

"Yeah." The tears began flowing more freely. "How are we supposed to make it through today?"

"I don't know, Colleen. I don't know." He swallowed hard. "Whitney loved birthdays."

"More her friends than her own. She always shot out the door on a mission every time a friend had a birthday." Both pictured Whitney running toward her car, a gift bag in one hand, car keys in the other. Neither wanted to move.

"I never knew I could hurt this bad," Newell said.

"Are you guys ready?" Carly asked as Newell and Colleen finally came downstairs.

"More than you know," Colleen said. Although it felt as though she had even more to do this day than the day before, she could not wait for their family time of shutting out the world and focusing on God in worship. "I really need this today," she said as she sat down.

Newell sat down on the couch next to his wife. "My only regret about this morning worship time is that it wasn't my idea," he said. "I guess no one will hold that against me."

"Don't be so sure, Dad," Carly joked. Just as she had the day before, Carly put a CD into the stereo and started the family worship time with music. Everyone sang, feeling the presence of the Lord filling the room. They then spent time reading aloud passages from the Bible, especially the book of Psalms, and praying. The time wasn't structured. They moved back and forth between these three elements. The four of them—Newell, Colleen, Carly, and Sandra—all knew they needed the strength and peace only God could provide, or they would never survive this day. Or the one to come.

Once again, the moment they pulled the sign off the door after their family worship time, the house exploded with activity. A group of Whitney's friends came by to finish projects they'd started the day before. Several had gathered their photographs of Whitney and themselves and placed them on large posters that would be displayed at the funeral home during the viewing. Sandra was right in the middle of all the activity, helping to add just the right touch to each poster.

Newell and Colleen's extended family had come into town from all over the country. Friends within the church had volunteered to provide places for them all to stay, which meant the Cerak's relatives were now spread throughout Gaylord. Many dropped by the house prior to going to the funeral home.

By twelve-thirty Newell and Colleen were out the door and off to the funeral home. Both knew it would be a long day, but they were anxious to get it under way. Carly and Sandra arrived a little while later. "Mom," Carly said, "have you ever seen so many flowers in your life?!"

"They just keep going and going, don't they?" Colleen said. The funeral home had three rooms that they used for both viewings and funerals. All three were filled to overflowing with flowers for Whitney. Along the wall of one room stood a row of easels, upon which rested the posters Whitney's friends had made. In the center of the far wall of the main room sat Whitney's casket. On top of it was a large floral arrangement and on a stand next to it was a picture of Whitney. The Ceraks walked over to the casket together. Newell placed his hand on it. "I can't believe she is in there," he said.

"But it's just her body, Dad," Carly said. "Whitney is in the presence of God right now, having the best birthday party anyone could ever imagine."

"I know, Carly. I know. If that wasn't true, this day would be unbearable."

Although the viewing wasn't scheduled to begin until two, a group of Whitney's friends, including her boyfriend, Matt, arrived early and gathered around her casket. Matt and another friend, Kyle, read poems they'd written for her, and everyone started sobbing. As Carly watched the scene from the other side of the room, she thought, *I never really knew how many people loved my little sister until now.*

At two a line formed as Newell, Colleen, and Carly took their place next to Whitney's casket. One by one, those who knew and loved Whitney walked up, hugged the Ceraks, and expressed their deepest sympathy. From time to time laughter would rise up from the corner of the room where people were watching the video-tapes of Whitney. Not only had the family decided to show videos of her previous birthdays, they'd also included some of the crazy videos Whitney and her friends had made when they'd stayed up all night at slumber parties. At one point the laughter became so loud that Newell turned toward the sound, smiling. "That's just

Whitney being Whitney on those tapes," he said. "I'm glad we brought those videos. Even now she's adding life to the room, just like she always did."

The laughter from the tapes set the mood the family wanted in the funeral home that Saturday afternoon. One woman who came through the line looked at Colleen and said, "I don't know how you can be so strong at a time like this."

"It's all from the Lord. Believe me, I could never do this on my own."

The woman gave Colleen a hug and said, "Lord bless you." Many of the others who came through the line shared stories with the Ceraks of specific ways in which Whitney had touched their lives. Over and over Newell and Colleen found themselves saying, "Thank you so much for sharing that with me. I had never heard that story before." Hearing others' memories of Whitney gave the Ceraks an extra boost of encouragement. They drew strength from those going through the line. They also tried to offer encouragement back. As people introduced themselves, it would often trigger a memory for Newell and Colleen, which they would then share.

The Ceraks were determined to celebrate the impact Whitney's life had had rather than dwell on that which would never be because she was gone. There would be plenty of time for the latter when the services were over and life tried to return to normal.

Some time around five, Jim Mathis walked over to Newell and Colleen and pulled them to the side. "I need to talk to you," he said.

"Can't it wait, Jim?" Colleen said. "The line goes out the door and around the building. It looks like the line for Space Mountain at Disney World. Some of these people have been waiting in line over an hour to speak to us."

"Exactly," Jim said. "There are so many people that this is going to last for a long, long time. You two need to take a break. Let Carly and Sandra handle the people for a while. Come on back to the lounge area. Get something to drink and grab a bite to eat."

"We're fine, Jim," Newell said. "If we get too tired, we'll take a break."

"I know better than that. As long as there are people in this line, you two will be right here, especially you, Colleen. Now, come on. I won't take no for an answer."

Newell and Colleen went with him to a small private room in the funeral home and sat down. Although they opened two bottles of water, neither of them ate any of the food sitting on the counter. Nor could they relax. Colleen's leg kept twitching, and Newell continually looked at his watch. After less than five minutes Newell looked over at his wife and said, "Are you ready to get back in there?"

"Let's go," Colleen said.

They walked back and took their place next to Whitney's casket. The last guest did not leave until after nine P.M., even though the visitation was scheduled to end at eight. Only then did Newell and Colleen eat something. Yet neither felt tired. Newell told Colleen, "None of this seems real. I feel like I am outside of my body watching someone else go through this." Colleen felt the same way.

When they returned home, they found their house was filled with Whitney's friends from both high school and college, along with many of Carly's friends. The two groups of friends didn't know one another. However, Carly saw this as a unique opportunity to bring them together. As they had the night before, Newell and Colleen went to sleep to the sound of their daughters' friends singing praises to God in their basement.

Death is Satan's greatest way to attack this world. Amazingly, then God takes what Satan uses to attack us and uses it to bring us together and reveal Himself the most. Through Satan's greatest strength, God's power still overcomes and is stronger.

Kelly and Carly, Rm. 110

Carly's journal entry, May 11, 2006

10

TURNING A CORNER

Thursday, May 4, 2006

Here's the latest on Laura's condition. They have reduced her dependence upon the ventilator now that they believe her body can handle more of the burden of breathing. They were providing 12 breaths a minute and backed it down to 6 breaths a minute. She handled that so well that they reduced it to 2 breaths a minute. This means that her body is making up the difference and she is breathing quite regularly now.

They connected the feeding tube to her stomach yesterday and her body is handling that very well! They had physical therapists evaluating her condition today. It was mostly just an evaluation of her abilities and limitations. They moved her to a special chair that allows her to sit up in a slightly reclined condition. The plan was to have her in that for about two hours today. Although she is still in the coma, they are trying to start her rehabilitation as quickly as possible. However, she was not responding to commands today, which reminds us of the doctor's comments that this may be more like a marathon than a sprint. I know we are hoping it's more like a mini-marathon, or a 5K, so please continue to pray for God's healing hand to wake Laura from this coma soon.

The neurologists were quite positive yesterday after doing a brain scan and examining her. There is no bleeding from the brain and they were comfortable enough with her condition to remove her cranial pressure sensor from her head. The family is very pleased with her care thus far and there is one doctor who has really taken ownership of Laura's case and is working closely with Laura and the Van Ryns.

BLOG ENTRY POSTED BY LISA VAN RYN ONE WEEK AFTER THE ACCIDENT

Susie gasped as she walked into Laura's room. *This can't be right! What have they done to her?* Laura was not lying in her bed as she had been every day since the accident. Her nurse had placed her in a chair. All of the tubes and wires still ran from her body to the various machines around the room; the ventilator tube protruded out of the tracheal tube and an IV tube ran to her arm, but she was sitting up. Still unconscious, eyes closed, but sitting up. Susie started to panic. She wanted to shout to the nurse, "*No!* You're going to hurt her. She needs to lie still so she can get better. What are you thinking, putting her in a chair like that? You aren't helping her. You're torturing her. How could you be so cruel?"

Reading Susie's thoughts in her eyes, the nurse said, "The body heals faster when we get people up and moving around. Even though Laura's unconscious, it helps to familiarize her body with different positions. Yes, she needs rest, but she needs more than that to completely recover."

"But," Susie stammered, "she's too . . ." She wasn't sure if she finished her sentence or merely thought it . . . *she's too fragile.*

"The body is really amazing and very resilient," the nurse told her. "I know this is hard for you to see. You probably don't want to be in here when we put her back into bed." The nurse was right. Susie wanted to know everything that the medical staff was doing to her daughter, but she didn't want to see it up close.

A few minutes after she returned to the waiting room, Lisa walked in and asked, "How is Laura this morning?"

"You're not going to believe this, but they had her up in a chair," Susie said.

"What?" Lisa said, walking straight to Laura's room to talk to the nurse. She didn't go back to complain about her sister's care, but to learn the hows and whys behind what the hospital staff did for her. A few days later, when Laura's physical and developmental therapies began, Lisa was right there beside her. She wanted to understand everything that was taking place.

Lisa and Susie noticed a marked change when they walked into Laura's room after the nurses had moved her back to her bed. The sedation from her surgery that had kept her so still throughout Tuesday and most of the day Wednesday had worn off. While still comatose, she was becoming more active. "She can't keep her right leg still." Lisa said, smiling. "That's just like Laura, always fidgeting. She never could keep that leg still when she was sitting or lying down."

Laura had thrashed around so much that it had led to an awkward positioning of the standard hospital gown. "I think she's tired of being in the bed. She's acting like she wants to get up. I hope she doesn't remember this, because she would really be embarrassed right now," Susie said as she threw the sheet back over her daughter. She and Lisa were glad there weren't any men in the room right then. When Laura immediately kicked the sheet off again, Lisa reached down to pull the hospital gown back down over her sister. That's when she noticed something odd. "What's that on her stomach? I've never noticed that before."

Susie wasn't sure what Lisa was talking about until she pointed directly to the spot right over Laura's navel. "That. It looks like she had her belly button pierced."

"I don't think so."

"Look at it. I'm telling you, that's not from the accident. That's a body piercing. She went out and got her belly button pierced. I wonder when she did that?"

"Are you sure?" Susie asked. She inspected the spot a little closer before Laura's body jerked to the side. "That's not like her, to do something like that without telling any of us."

"Maybe we ought to check her for tattoos," Lisa said. "Girl turns twenty-one, and she thinks she can do whatever she wants." Susie didn't find her comment amusing.

The conversation abruptly ended when Laura began making a gurgling sound through the tracheal tube, as if she were choking. "Nurse, nurse!" Susie called out.

Bri, one of the ICU nurses, came over and asked, "What's wrong, Mrs. Van Ryn?"

"It sounds like she's about to choke to death."

"Let me have a look," Bri said. All the doctors, nurses, and staff at Parkview went above and beyond the call of duty in caring for Laura, but twenty-five-year-old Bri was unique. She cared for Laura as if she were her own sister. One day she even surprised the Van Ryns by braiding Laura's hair into two pigtails, which the family loved. "She's all right," Bri said as she suctioned the fluid out of the tube. "That's normal with a respirator. If you would like, I can show you how to suction the fluid out yourself."

Susie swallowed hard. "No, thank you." Lisa, however, took Bri up on her offer and also showed her brothers the procedure.

From then on, whenever one of her children or a nurse started working on the ventilator tubes, Susie left the room. The sound of

Laura gurgling on her own fluids filled her with the fear that her daughter might choke and die. She also left the room any time a nurse gave Laura a shot or fed a new IV line into her veins. Every time they poked Laura, Susie felt it. She couldn't stand the thought of all the pain being inflicted on her little girl.

Although Susie struggled with the sounds of Laura's choking and the wooshing as the ventilator breathed for her, she tried to tell herself that it was helping Laura. The hospital had reduced the number of breaths the ventilator made for Laura from twelve to six and finally down to two. She did the rest of her breathing on her own, which was an encouraging sign, the first of many that were to come over the next few days.

Laura's latest CAT scan had shown no signs of bleeding, so her doctor had removed the spike. She also showed more signs of trying to wake up. She appeared to try to open her eyes more frequently, especially in response to the sound of her family's voices. Her body accepted the feeding tube, and her color continued to improve, along with her breathing. Her improvements also allowed therapists to begin the early stages of occupational therapy. This meant putting Laura in a chair more often and stimulating her muscles. And above all, she showed no signs of pneumonia, which is nearly unheard of for someone on a respirator as long as Laura had been.

Aside from where they'd shaved her head for the cranial pressure sensor, Laura's head and face now looked nearly normal. To her mother, she looked beautiful. Susie loved to sit and stare at her daughter as she slept. Even though Laura could not communicate in any way, and even though she never gave any sign of knowing anyone was in the room with her, that didn't matter to Susie. The fact that her daughter was alive was enough. Susie prayed that this coma was God's gift to Laura, to spare her from the pain that racked her body, and to allow her to heal. "I want to think that God is letting you sleep so you can physically heal without so much pain," Susie whispered to her daughter as she sat next to her bed, holding her hand. "You are opening your eyes slightly and we think you may be following our voices with your eyes. Oh, Laura, can you hear me? Don't get frustrated. God will wake you up soon. We're resting in His care." She patted her daughter's arm. "God gave me this verse for you today. Psalm 29:11 says, 'The Lord gives strength to His people; the Lord blesses His people with peace.' I'm praying that God gives you peace from the pain and brings you back to us very soon."

Aryn tapped on the door. "Do you mind if I come in?" he asked.

"No, not at all," Susie replied. Both she and Don knew how hard it was for Aryn to sit in the waiting room with the crowd. He tried to grab every moment he could with Laura while at the same time being sensitive to the fact that he wasn't yet an official part of the family. "I was just getting ready to leave, so you walked in at just the right time. Stay as long as you like," Susie said as she left the room.

Aryn sat down next to Laura and took her hand. "I wish I knew that you could hear me and that you know I am here," he said as tears welled up in his eyes. "Oh, babe, I miss you so bad. I keep asking God to let you open your eyes and wake up. I have so much to tell you." He paused and stared deeply at her. Memories from their three years together flashed through his mind. Try as he might, he couldn't also help but wonder if they would have any more.

He also battled the what-ifs, especially after Laura's best friend, Sara, told him that Laura almost did not ride in the Taylor van on the night of the accident. Sara had driven her own car to Fort Wayne to work the banquet, and Laura, Brad, and Whitney had gone with her. Sara and Whitney's sister, Carly, were close friends, which was why Sara had invited Whitney to ride with them. Brad kept them all entertained on the drive up, telling one joke after another. After the banquet, Sara did not return to school with everyone else. Instead, she drove up to her home in Michigan. She was getting married right after graduation and needed to work on the wedding plans. Laura had given serious thought to driving up to Detroit with Sara and surprising Aryn with a visit, but for whatever reason, she decided to stay at school. Perhaps with graduation bearing down on her, she needed to get back to Taylor to finish her final projects. Aryn had spent the previous weekend in Upland visiting Laura at school. He kept thinking, *What if I hadn't? What if I hadn't gone to visit her, then she might have come on up and surprised me and she wouldn't have been in that van.*

He pushed the thoughts out of his head. "Our time together last weekend was amazing," he whispered to her. "Nothing was left unsaid. If that had to be our last time together for a while, that's okay. We had so much fun. You left me with some great memories to hold me over until we can make new ones." He glanced down at her toes on her right foot and thought about watching her paint her toenails the Sunday before the accident. Aryn smiled. *Her nail polish is still the same color. She didn't change it between Sunday and the time of the accident,* he thought to himself. The thought made him feel even more connected to her, if that was possible. He took hold of Laura's hand and asked her to squeeze his finger if she knew he was there. She did. Aryn could hardly contain his joy.

Monday, May 8, 2006

Last night our family was able to attend the memorial service held at the Taylor University campus for the 5 people who lost their lives in this accident. We were encouraged by the testimonies of those families and to hear how God has been working in the lives of so many through this situation. We would ask you today to continue to uphold the families in prayer (the families of Whitney Cerak, Laurel Erb, Monica Felver, Brad Larson, and Betsy Smith). And rejoice with them as well, that those dear children of God are not dead today but alive and in the presence of our Lord and Savior, Jesus Christ! We continue to see encouraging signs from Laura today as she is now breathing entirely on her own. They have removed the respirator and she is breathing through the trach at what the nurse called "a very normal rate." Again this morning they had her sitting in a chair and she's been looking pretty peaceful so far today.

Blog entry posted by Lisa Van Ryn

As the days at Parkview advanced, the Van Ryns' world moved between short nights at the Samaritan's House and long days in the waiting room of the ICU. Don and Susie's only uninterrupted time with their daughter came first thing in the morning. Most days, the hospital staff would let them go back to see her between 8:15 and 8:30. Aryn would arrive around the same time, and Lisa, Mark, and Kenny would come over to the hospital a little later. After their initial visit with Laura, it was back to the waiting room and filling their time with reading, playing card games and jigsaw puzzles, and playing host to the crowds that would gather each day. People brought food for the family nearly every day. Two or three times during their stay the owner of a local pub brought over doughnuts and milk. As the day wore on, more food would arrive. The family stocked up on paper plates and plastic forks, spoons, and knives, filling the waiting room cabinets with their stash.

One morning Don walked into the waiting room after a prolonged time with Laura. He glanced around, then said to no one in particular, "Must be the weekend."

"Oh, yeah, DV, what was your first clue?" Lisa said, laughing.

"Are any students left on campus at Taylor, because I think they are all here right now," he said. "You know the drill. I guess we get to line them up and usher them back, in about an hour."

"Where's Suz and Aryn?" Lisa asked. "Are they both still back with Laura?"

"Your mom is. Aryn went for a walk. I don't think he much cares for the crowds in here," he said.

"He's trying," Lisa said. The conversation was interrupted when Don's brother, Dave, and his wife, Ruthann, walked in.

"How is she today?" Dave asked.

"She's doing okay, but there's a long way to go. If you want, I can take you back right now," Don said.

"No, we can wait until the regular visiting hours," his brother said.

"Nah, I'll take you back now. Family can go back anytime they want."

Don led his brother and sister-in-law back to Laura's room. Susie stood up from beside Laura's bed and hugged Ruthann. "She looks a lot better now than when they first brought her in. The doctors are talking about moving her out of ICU and up to a regular room."

"That's great, that's really great. I know we've been praying for her, and we've got everyone we know praying for her," Dave said.

Ruthann didn't say much. She stood near Susie and gave her another hug when they left the room after only a few minutes. When they returned to the waiting room, Lisa walked over to them and said, "This may be hard to believe, but she looks really great compared to when they first brought her in here."

Ruthann scrunched up her face like she'd bitten into something sour. "I don't care what anyone says, that doesn't look like Laura to me."

Lisa gave a little laugh. "If you'd been through what she's been through, you wouldn't look like yourself either," she said.

Tuesday, May 9, 2006

It's a beautiful sunny day again here in Fort Wayne, and we have some encouraging signs from Laura to share with you today. She has been stretching and moving around quite a bit. The doctor lifted her eyelids and Laura seems to be trying to focus her eyes a little bit more. Her trademark "shaking of the leg" was in full effect this morning, and she was even snapping her fingers when we asked her to!

While these little signs keep us encouraged we realize that this road is going to be a long one. Keep praying that the Lord would give her the peace and comfort that she needs as she slowly wakes up and begins to understand where she is and what's happening. This afternoon they are doing an MRI on her head and another on her spine to make sure it's all right to remove her neck brace (which has only been there for precautionary measures). They plan to move Laura to the 7th floor today, where she will have her own room and we will be able to spend a lot more time with her. That will be nice.

Blog entry posted by Lisa Van Ryn

On May 9 Laura was moved from the ICU into a double room on the seventh floor in the neurology wing, but she did not have a roommate. A nurse suggested that someone stay with Laura for the first night or two. "However," she told the family, "you need to limit it to only one or two people at a time. Laura's starting to become more aware of her surroundings as she's waking up. Her senses will also become hypersensitive. We need to be careful that we do not overstimulate her. That also means limiting who comes in to see her. Until she wakes up, we need to keep it to immediate family only."

"Don't worry, we will," Don said. Once the nurse had left the room, Don said, "Okay, your mother and I will take the first night. Who wants to be next?"

A short time later a woman walked into the seventh-floor lounge area and introduced herself. "My name is Joelle," she said, "and I will be one of Laura's therapists. I know she's not fully awake yet, but that's okay. I will work with her to not only try to get some of her muscle memory back, but to also help get the neurons firing in her brain. That's how the brain heals itself from an injury like this."

"How much can you get her to do at this stage?" Susie asked.

"Oh, you would be surprised," Joelle said. She walked into Laura's room with Don, Susie, and Lisa in tow. "We will start with something really basic like brushing her teeth. I know she can't stand up over a sink, put toothpaste on her brush, and brush them like you and me, but it's the basic motion we want to reacquaint her with." Turning to Laura she said, "Okay, sweetheart, how would you like to brush your teeth today?" She placed the toothbrush into her hand.

Laura did not respond. However, she did begin to purse her lips and move her tongue on them as if they were bothering her. "I think she wants her ChapStick," Lisa said. "Laura always had ChapStick handy."

"If you have some, go ahead and give it to her," Joelle said.

Lisa put the tube in her sister's hand. Without opening her eyes, Laura rubbed her hands over it, flipped it right side up, pulled off the cap, and brushed it over her lips. Lisa and Susie looked at one another and let out big grins. "That's Laura," Susie said to Joelle. "She can't stand for her lips to feel dry. I used to joke that she could put on ChapStick in her sleep. I guess she really can."

II

A CELEBRATION OF LIFE

I feel so blessed that I was able to watch [Whitney's] love for God and her desire to know Him become so real. She had fallen in love with Him. So God answered my deepest prayer. And I am in no way sad for Whitney. She had a full life for only nineteen years. That's pretty incredible.

God has blessed me more than I can imagine. He gave me the best friend I could have ever asked for and the best nineteen years of my life. And through her death, the love and power of Jesus has been made so real to me because I am weak and in pain, but He is carrying me and my family. And these are not just words that help me feel better and help me cope with my loss. I know the living God, and, just like Whitney underlined in her Bible, my soul yearns and even faints for Him. He is my hope because of His unbelievable love. I will someday be in front of Him—next to my sister.

CARLY, SPOKEN AT WHITNEY'S FUNERAL

The Ceraks awoke Sunday morning with a sense of finality. All the activity of the past few days would culminate in Whitney's funeral. They'd planned the service with their pastor and arranged for Joshua, their church's worship leader, to lead everyone in singing several of Whitney's favorite songs. Instead of having the church's worship band play, they had asked Carly's boyfriend, Ben, to play the piano and one of Whitney's friends, Alysha, to sing backup. Newell, Carly, and Sandra all planned to speak, along with Mark Vaporis and Whitney's boyfriend, Matt. Pastor Jim Mathis would deliver the primary message. Because the family wanted to hold the funeral in the church, all of the flowers and posters and everything else that had filled the funeral home would be delivered to the church between the end of the worship services and the beginning of the funeral.

Now all the family had to do was wait. The last of their relatives had arrived on Saturday, and friends had volunteered to take them to church that morning, which gave the Ceraks and Sandra some time alone. After so much noise and so many people over the past two days, they needed it. The calm was short-lived, however. Friends from out of town dropped by the house and were welcomed inside, which cut the family's worship time short.

As soon as their worship time ended, Carly retreated upstairs to write out what she wanted to say at her sister's funeral. She sat on her bed and tapped her pen against the legal pad. Carly had to force herself to believe this was really happening. Every time she looked up from her paper, she expected to see her sister come charging through her door, a big, dimpled smile on her face.

"Whitney and I have had quite the relationship," she wrote. "When we were younger we didn't really get along, mostly because I was a little brat." Two and a half pages later, she folded the paper and started getting ready to leave for the church.

When Colleen went to get dressed, she looked through her closet and asked out loud to no one in particular, "How do people find the time to go shopping before a funeral? Where do they find those great black outfits they wear?" Newell started to answer, but thought better of it. He walked out and one of her friends came in.

"I don't know what I am going to wear!" Colleen said. She pulled one thing after another out of her closet, tried them on, then pulled out something else. Finally she and her friend settled on a black dress hanging in the back of her closet. Newell came back upstairs and started getting ready as well. As he tied his tie and Colleen put on her makeup, she glanced over at him and said, "Are you okay?"

"Aside from the fact that I'm getting ready for my daughter's funeral, I'm doing great," he said with an ironic laugh.

Before they knew it, it was after twelve. The family loaded up in the car together and drove to the church. They wanted to make sure every detail was ready before they started another visitation time for those who had been unable to come to the funeral home the night before. A long line of mourners was waiting for them as soon as they arrived shortly after twelve: By 1:45 the funeral director cut off the line. It was time for Newell, Colleen, Carly, and Sandra to take their places. Fifteen minutes later they walked into the auditorium behind Whitney's casket, hand in hand. Over fourteen hundred people packed the church, with the overflow crowd spilling into the foyer.

The Ceraks took their seats in the front row of the church as Mark Vaporis, one of the church's associate pastors, said to the crowd, "Thank you for coming today. And, on behalf of the family, we appreciate each and every one of you and the great outpouring of love that is very evident here." Mark's voice cracked, and he could barely continue speaking. Newell grabbed Colleen's hand. "This is it," he whispered.

As the service began, Colleen waited for the inevitable. Kleenex in hand, she waited for the breakdown she thought was coming. But it never came. It didn't come as Matt stood and talked about how Whitney was his best friend and he didn't know what he would do without her. It didn't come as Sandra told how she and Whitney hadn't liked each other when they first met. "Whitney thought I had told her mother that she liked a boy when we were in the fourth grade, which was the worst thing one fourth-grade girl could do to another" Sandra explained. Colleen laughed along with everyone else. The breakdown did not arrive.

Nor did the breakdown come as Carly stood and described how deeply Whitney loved the people around her, and how she would go to those in pain and cry with them. Rather than break down, Colleen sat and admired both her daughters. As Carly talked of how Whitney always lit up a room, Colleen couldn't help but think how Carly herself brought that light into the church auditorium as she spoke of her sister.

And finally, the breakdown did not come as Newell spoke longer than all the previous speakers combined. Colleen laughed with the rest of the crowd as he described Whitney bouncing off to her first day of school, wearing a pink jacket and purple hat and backpack. He told how Whit came home that first day, a huge smile on her face, and he knew she would be okay. "I knew that her school career would not be a problem for her. She could handle just about anything. Just flash that smile, tilt her head, give that look, pout her lips, and she could win her way into your heart," he said. As he did, Colleen could see Whitney. That smile. That look. It was if her daughter were right there with her again, and the thought filled her with joy.

Carly took in the entire experience. *I cannot believe so many people are here.* Glancing around, she noticed a large Taylor University section, with students, professors, and staff. She'd seen the bus in the parking lot with the words "Indiana Wesleyan University" painted on the side. IWU is located less than twenty miles from Taylor, and the schools are each other's biggest rivals. A friend had told Carly that Taylor was sending out busloads of people to the funerals of all of the accident victims, and that IWU supplied buses when Taylor did not have enough for all the people.

After Mark's opening remarks, Joshua walked up onto the stage and led the crowd in worship. Tears began flowing down Carly's cheeks as she sang, "How great is our God . . ." *Whitney loved that song,* she remembered. In spite of the tears, she found it easy to worship the Lord. *O God,* she prayed, *you are so near right now. I need your strength. O God, I need your strength.* As soon as the music stopped, she walked up on the platform with Sandra, Newell, and Matt. Matt spoke first and could barely make it through the remarks he'd prepared. *Hold him up, Lord,* Carly prayed. *You can get him through this.* Then Sandra spoke. Carly beamed. *She really has become a sister,* she thought as she listened to Sandra describe her relationship with Whitney and the entire Cerak family.

Then it was Carly's turn. She pulled out the paper on which

she'd written what she wanted to say, and started reading. All day she'd feared she would fall apart in the middle and not be able to finish. Yet as she spoke, she felt a strength she'd never felt before. As her mouth read the words on the page, she almost felt as though someone else was speaking and she was sitting back listening. "I watched my sister begin to love God with all her heart," she read. "I feel so blessed that I was able to watch her love for God grow and her desire for Him become so real. She had fallen in love with Him. So God answered my deepest prayer. And I am in no way sad for Whitney—she had a full life for only nineteen years, and that's pretty incredible." When Carly finished speaking, she let out a sigh and a prayer, and stood back as her father spoke.

Newell felt compelled to speak at his daughter's funeral. He had to do it. More than anything he wanted everyone who was there to know the real Whitney and how passionately she loved her God. Like Carly, he felt a strength that he knew came from the Lord. His voice cracked in places, and once or twice he thought he might not make it through, but then the moment passed.

"I miss her. We all miss her," he said. "But knowing she was becoming a woman of God makes it a little easier to take . . . Now she is in the presence of her King. She is worshipping and glorifying Him today. She found the answers to those hard questions [that people ask at funerals], and that answer is Christ. Who is it that keeps us strong to deal with this tragedy? She understood and she was making Christ her own. She was leaning on Him. She believed absolutely in Christ's love, that love that took Him to the cross for her—*for us.*

"This is why we do not grieve as the world grieves," he continued. "It hurts. We miss her. But it is not despair that drowns us. We, like Whit, have the faith and trust believing God's words as true, and that one day we will be reunited. I fully, fully believe that. It's not a fantasy. It is not some wish. I believe it with all my heart. I believe it with all my heart."

At one point Newell said, "I apologize for speaking so long, but Whitney is my daughter, so I plan on taking as much time as I want." The crowd laughed with approval. He concluded by saying, "I love my daughter, and I know that she is going to be missed, but the thing that I really want you to know about her life is that she found that Jesus Christ is the answer. And only He can console. And only He can give hope. And only He can wash our sins away. It is only by God's grace that we bear up under all this tragedy. God is real, and Whitney knows it. And our prayer is that you know this Christ that is Whitney's Savior, Lord, and King. Her almost nineteen years were full, but I know Whit would tell you that the most important thing was this last year when Christ became so real for her. And it is her desire for you, too, to know Him as Lord and Savior and King." After speaking, he took his place next to Colleen, who put her arm around him. Neither said a word.

After Newell, Jim Mathis stood and spoke. The Ceraks prayed for him because they knew this day was as hard on him as it was on the rest of the family. Jim had known Whitney since the day she was born. As Newell's best friend, he'd watched Whit grow up. He spoke, not as a professional minister giving a eulogy, but as a hurting friend who wanted more than anything to share the hope that drove Whitney, the hope of Jesus Christ.

Following the funeral service, the church held a dinner for the church family in the gymnasium. Tables spread out across the room, and each one was decorated with Whitney's favorite flower, Gerber daisies. Newell and Colleen were not able to sit down to eat for all the people who came up to them, telling them stories of Whitney, and assuring them that they were praying for them. At one point Colleen turned to Newell and said, "I know I should be a basket case by now, but I'm not. I don't know how to explain it."

"I know," Newell said, "I feel it too. It's like . . ."

"It's like God is in the room holding me up."

"Exactly."

Monday morning the family had to forgo its usual worship time. Several friends from Upland had come up for the funeral, and Newell and Colleen planned on meeting them for breakfast first thing in the morning. At breakfast, they immersed themselves in talking and laughing and catching up on the eighteen years since the Ceraks had moved from Upland to Gaylord. At one point Newell said to Colleen, "This doesn't exactly fit the picture of the day after our daughter's funeral, does it?" They enjoyed their time together with friends so much that Newell and Colleen lost track of time.

By the time they returned home from the restaurant it was already 10:30. Whitney's graveside service and burial was scheduled for eleven. Cars lined the street in front of their home and filled the driveway. Newell and Colleen rushed into the house, which was filled with family waiting for them. Although the funeral had been a public service, only family had been invited to the grave site. "Mom, we're going to be late," Carly called out.

"No, we won't. We'll make it. Besides, I don't think they will start the service without us," Colleen said. She and Newell ran upstairs, quickly got ready, and came back down. "All right, let's go," she said.

A load of people climbed into the Ceraks' car, and all the other cars surrounding the house filled up. Newell led the way to the cemetery, with the rest of their extended family following behind. They wound their way to Whitney's grave site. Right across the street were the soccer fields where Whitney had played many, many games growing up. As he climbed out of the car, Newell started looking around and taking inventory of everyone who was there. "Where's my mom?" he asked.

Colleen felt her heart drop through her shoes. She couldn't make a sound.

Newell found her silence surprising. He turned around and saw her mouth hanging wide open. "Colleen?" he said.

"Oh, no," she said. "We were supposed to go get her. She's staying at Yohe's cottage on Dixon Lake. I told her that we would pick her up at ten-thirty but I forgot to tell you."

Newell glanced at his watch and back up at the crowd of people walking over to the row of chairs next to the casket. The service was about to start and his mother was fifteen minutes away.

"What are we going to do?" Colleen asked.

"Let me talk it over with my brothers and sisters," Newell said. He walked over and asked, "Do you think Mom will mind if she's not here for this ceremony? It's not going to last but maybe five minutes. I was supposed to go get her, but in all the rush I completely forgot." The consensus among his brothers and sisters was that their mom would be more upset that they delayed the service to go get her. He walked back over to Colleen. "She'll be fine. Let's go ahead and start the service."

Jim led the service and read 1 Thessalonians 4:13-18:

> Brothers, we do not want you to be ignorant about those who fall asleep, or to grieve like the rest of men, who have no hope. We believe that Jesus died and rose again and so we believe that God will bring with Jesus those who have fallen asleep in him. According to the Lord's own word, we tell you that we who are still alive, who are left till the coming of the Lord, will certainly not precede those who have fallen asleep. For the Lord himself will come down from heaven, with a loud command, with the voice of the archangel and with the trumpet call of God, and the dead in Christ will rise first. After that, we who are still alive and are left will be caught up together with them in the clouds to meet the Lord in the air. And so we will be with the Lord forever. Therefore encourage each other with these words.

He then made a few short remarks, and led the group in prayer.

Newell had been right. The entire ceremony lasted five minutes at the most. After it was over, he arranged for someone else to take Colleen home and then drove out to Dixon Lake to pick up his mother. She and his sister Grace were staying there together. However, Grace had left earlier in the morning to take their brother Russ to the airport.

Newell pulled up to the front of the house, parked the car, and walked up on the porch. As he reached up to knock on the door, he looked through the window. His mother sat in a chair, her coat on, waiting for him to arrive. *She's probably been like that for an hour now, waiting patiently for me to show up.* He walked in the door and immediately said, "I am so sorry, Mom. Colleen is worried she's going to be demoted on the daughter-in-law list for forgetting you."

His mother laughed. "Newell, it's all right. Don't give it another thought."

"But, Mom, you missed Whitney's graveside service. I feel terrible about that."

"That's all right," she said in a way that only a mother can, "it doesn't really matter because it isn't really Whitney anyway."

Newell knew his mother's meaning. As a Christian, she knew Whitney's spirit—the real Whitney—was now in the presence of God. However, a few weeks later Newell would look back on his mother's words in a whole new light.

12

"HI"

Matthew 18:19–20: "Again, I tell you that if two of you on earth agree about anything you ask for, it will be done for you by my Father in heaven. For where two or three come together in my name, there am I with them."

I've been thinking about prayer. About asking the Father for things—and expecting Him to answer as He's promised to. You and I have been praying for Laura and asking God to heal her. We've come together, though far apart, in His name to ask Him to heal her. We were overwhelmed to read from Dave that over a thousand people may be daily checking this site to learn about how to best pray for Laura. So I was wondering if today we could, with one voice and one heart, cry out to the Father on Laura's behalf. Let's pray the following together, with expectant hearts knowing that our Heavenly Father knows all of our needs and all about Laura's life and body and what is best for her.

Dear Father, we praise you for being all knowing and indescribably good. We praise you for being the Living God—the only true God. We thank you and are humbled for the way you love us and care for us. We thank you again for sparing Laura's life and together, we ask you to heal her completely. Restore her to us in your time and give us strength as we wait. We completely trust in you and your perfect plans. May this experience be bringing many into closer relationships with you. You are a good God. We know that you can do so much more than anything we could ask or imagine. Thank you for what you're doing. Teach us how to crawl up into your lap and be Your children. Help us to love you and to love others. Watch over Laura today—we

know she is in your hands. We ask all of this in the name of our Lord and Savior, Jesus Christ. Amen. Let it be.
BLOG ENTRY POSTED BY LISA VAN RYN

"Did you hear that?" Don said. He grabbed Susie's hand and moved closer to Laura's bed. "Can you say it again, Laurie? Can you say 'hi'?"

Laura pressed her lips together, and in a gentle whisper, barely audible, she said, "Hi." It was her first spoken word in over two weeks.

Don jumped up with a big smile on his face while Susie cried. "Laurie, it's Mom. Can you tell me hi?"

"Hi," Laura said.

Tears poured down Susie's face. Her shoulders shook as she reached out and took Laura's hand. "Hi, sweetheart. Hi to you too."

"Hi," Laura said. Her eyes were closed, but she turned toward the sound of Don and Susie's voices. A couple of hours earlier a nurse had removed the ventilator tube and capped off the tracheotomy. With the tube gone and the trach capped, she could now breathe completely through her nose and mouth. The doctors said she might speak, and now she had.

"Hi," Laura said again.

"That's the sweetest sound I've ever heard," Susie said.

"The kids are going to be mad they missed this," Don said with a smile. "They should have stayed a little longer. She's starting to wake up, Suz. Our daughter is coming back to us."

"I hope so," Susie said as she held on to Laura's hand and

stared at her expressionless face. She reached down and stroked her daughter's blonde hair. "Wake up soon, sunshine girl. We're right here, waiting for you."

Don and Susie sat together by Laura's bedside for a long time, just watching her "sleep." She lay anything but still. Laura had become proficient at finding new ways to escape the clutches of the bed. "There she goes again," Don said as Laura began rolling around in the bed. "Why do I get the feeling she's trying to out-wit us?"

Susie chuckled. "It's like trying to sleep with her at the Chip-munk Inn." They both smiled at the memory of the family's cabin at the Upper Peninsula Bible Camp, named for the chipmunks that dart in and out around the porch. "That child would kick and squirm in her sleep so much, I would wake up bruised if I tried to sleep next to her."

Once Laura calmed down, Susie told Don, "Why don't you go get some sleep. I'll take the first shift tonight." Throughout Laura's time on the seventh floor, the family would take turns sit-ting up with her for two- or three-hour shifts.

"Okay. I will relieve you in a couple of hours," Don said as he walked over to the extra bed behind the divider curtain.

During Don's shift later that night, Laura became especially agitated. He walked over and tried to hold Laura's upper body to keep her from hitting her broken elbow against something and injuring it further. Before he knew it, she'd swung her legs around and scissor-wrapped them around his waist. Later he wrote in the blog, "I felt like I was wrestling an angel."

• • •

Early the next morning Don heard a stirring behind the curtain that divided the semiprivate room. Susie walked directly over to Laura's bed. "Good morning, sunshine girl."

"Good morning," Laura repeated softly. Susie flashed a huge grin to Don.

"Hi," Don said.

"Hi," Laura whispered.

"Can you say 'Pops'?"

"Pops." Laura's eyelids fluttered as if she was trying to open her eyes. She managed to open the left one just a little.

Don smiled from ear to ear. "That's right, Laurie. That's right," he said. "I've been waiting a long time to hear you say Pops."

A nurse walked in to check Laura's vitals. "Good morning, Laura. How are you this morning."

"Good morning," Laura repeated.

Don let out a huge grin. "She started talking last night. Told us hi. So far her vocabulary is up to three words, but we'll take it."

"You're doing great, Laura," Susie said as she rubbed her daughter's hand. "Keep trying, babe. Keep fighting. You are so strong. Keep fighting back."

A couple of hours later Joelle came into the room for Laura's first therapy session of the day. "And how is she today?"

"She said her first words," Susie said, smiling.

Joelle clapped her hands. "That's our girl." During her time working with Laura at Parkview, Joelle had grown very close to both Laura and the Van Ryn family. After one of Laura's earliest therapy sessions, Joelle had made a point of telling the family that she shared their faith and prayed for Laura daily. "Well, let's see what we can get you to do today, Laura," she said.

With Lisa's help, Joelle lifted Laura up to move her to a wheelchair. As they did, they allowed her to stand for a few moments on her strong leg. Joelle smiled. "She'll be doing a lot more of that on *both* legs before too long, you just wait and see," she said. After they secured Laura in the chair, Joelle said, "We can take her for a little stroll, if you want."

"Really?" Lisa said. "All right, here we go, Laur."

Laura moved closer to consciousness each day. She opened her eyes more often, but her gaze remained glassy. A few days earlier a doctor had opened one of her eyes and tried to get her to focus. "She probably has double vision," the doctor told the family.

As Lisa rolled her sister down the hallway with Joelle in tow behind, Laura opened one eye, then the other. Occasionally she would open both, but primarily she opened her left eye. "It's a beautiful day today," Joelle said. "Why don't we take her outside?"

"She should enjoy that," Lisa said. "She hasn't been outside since she arrived here."

"Then it's time she goes. Besides, she needs a variety of stimulations to get the neurons firing again. However, we'll definitely want to put some sunglasses on her. It's pretty bright today."

From time to time as they rolled down the hall toward the door, Laura would move her foot and leg as if she was trying to help push the wheelchair. "That's it," Lisa said, "yeah, that's really good." They reached the door, and Lisa placed her sunglasses on

Laura, and made sure she was covered with the small blanket they'd brought along.

Once outside, they wheeled Laura over to a small fountain in the hospital courtyard. "Let's try something," Joelle said. She placed Laura's toe in the water and asked her, "How do you like that?"

"Cold," Laura said with that very hoarse, very whispery voice.

"Would you like to take your foot out?" Lisa asked. Laura nodded. "That's awesome," Lisa said with a smile.

They stayed outside for a little while longer. The sun shone brightly, a perfect May day in Indiana. Soon Laura began pulling at her shirt. "I wonder what that means?" Lisa said as she looked to Joelle for an answer. Laura kept tugging at her shirt, a look of obvious aggravation on her face. "Are you hot?" Lisa asked.

Laura nodded.

Lisa smiled. "Do you want to go inside?"

Again, Laura nodded.

"Okay, let's go back inside," Lisa said, still smiling. It was the closest thing to a conversation she'd had with her sister since the accident. She and Joelle wheeled Laura back to her room and moved her back into her bed. The head of the bed was raised in a sitting position. "Would you like to sit up or lie down?" Lisa asked.

"Down," Laura replied.

"Whatever you want," Lisa said. She turned to Joelle and said, "This is great. She's doing great today."

"There's still a long way to go, but this has been a really good day," Joelle said.

The next night Don thought Chinese food sounded good. The nurses recommended a nearby restaurant, and he went by and picked up a variety of dishes. When he returned, he spread the white containers out on a shelf beside the extra bed in Laura's room, and the smell filled the room. When the rest of the family came in, they closed the curtain between the beds and tried to eat quietly.

About halfway through the meal, Don paused and asked, "Did you hear that?"

"What?" Lisa said.

"Listen," Don said. He heard the sound again. "I think Laura just said something." He slipped out from behind the curtain and walked over to Laura. A moment later he came back, laughing.

"What?" Susie asked.

"She said it stinks," Don said.

"You're kidding me," Susie said.

"No. She whispered it real soft, just one word. 'Stinks,' she said." The entire family burst out laughing, then caught themselves.

"Shhhhh," Don said, then chuckled. "I guess the doctors were right. I remember they said her brain injury will make her senses overly sensitive. I guess eating Chinese food in her room wasn't such a good idea." He laughed and took another bite. "Too late now," he said. "Might as well finish it off."

Wednesday, May 17, 2006

Laura rested very well last night and Dad got a "good morning" out of her today. She had one more scan this morning, and all the doctors have cleared her to move. They also took the trach out this morning. She is scheduled to be transported to Grand Rapids by ambulance tomorrow morning at 9:00 A.M. There she will be enrolled in an excellent comprehensive rehab program. That facility is fairly close to home for us, close to friends, to a nice deli and best of all to one of our favorite ice cream places. So, after three weeks, it looks like we're finally heading home. Please pray for safe travel for us tomorrow. We've got four family vehicles here that we'll be driving home as well. Pray specifically that Laura will do well on the trip. Fort Wayne has been good to us. We've made a lot of friends here at the hospital and in the community. We've been well taken care of through this time and we're grateful for that. While it will be great to get home, we'll miss the people here. Thanks, FW, for taking care of Laura and us. We remain in His good care.

Blog entry posted by Lisa Van Ryn

"Are you okay over there, Suz? I don't think you've exhaled since we got in the car," Don said as they followed the ambulance out of the Parkview Hospital parking lot.

"I will be fine once we get there," she said.

"They wouldn't have okayed moving her if she couldn't handle the trip," Don said.

"I know, I know, but what if something goes wrong? I'm ready to get home, but I don't like the idea of moving her be-

◀ Cerak family, Easter 2006: Carly, Newell, Colleen, Sandra, Whitney

▶ Whitney and her friends at Taylor University, December 2005: Emily, Amy, Anne, Whitney

◀ Van Ryn family, summer 2004: Laura, Mark, Susie, Don, Kenny, Lisa

▶ Laura and her roommates at Taylor University, spring 2005: Brittney, Laura, Sara, Christine, Courtney, "The Apt!"

◀ Spring break 2006: Brittney, Jordan, Brad, Laura, Sara, Christine

▲ Spring break 2006: Laura Van Ryn and Brad Larson

▲ Laura and her camp friends, November 2004

▲ Laura and her boyfriend, Aryn, summer 2005

▶ Summer 2004: Laura, Kenny, Mark, and Lisa Van Ryn

Whitney in the intensive care unit at Parkview Hospital, Fort Wayne, Indiana, April 2006, in a comatose state

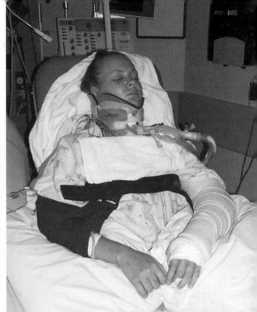

Accident site, I-69, Indiana, April 26, 2006

Whitney and her dog, Hunter, reunited

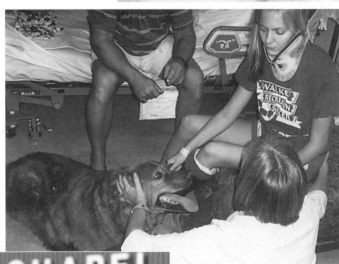

REDIGER CHAPEL

Taylor students gathered to pray on evening of April 26, 2006

◀ Whitney with physical therapists at Spectrum CCC, Grand Rapids, June 2006

▼ Whitney with occupational therapists Michelle and Carrie at Spectrum CCC, Grand Rapids, June 2006

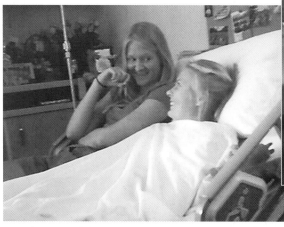

▲ Lisa and Whitney with therapist Joelle, from Parkview Hospital, April 2007

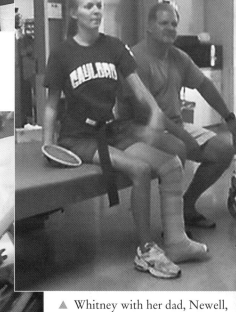

▲ Whitney with her sister Carly at Spectrum CCC, June 2006

▲ Whitney with her dad, Newell, during physical therapy session, Spectrum CCC

Dr. Martin Waalkes, neuropsychologist at Hope
etwork, August 2007 visit

▲ Whitney, Holly, Tia, Sandra,
Heather, fall 2006

◀ Whitney with friends Holly and
Emily, Grand Rapids, summer 2006

▲ Whitney and Carly Cerak,
Christmas 2006

◀ Whitney with her boyfriend, Matt,
and her sister Sandra at Spring Hill
Camp, July 2006

◀ Whitney with her mom, Colleen Cerak (*right*), and Susie Van Ryn (*left*), April 2007

▶ Whitney with her dad, Newell Cerak (*right*), and Don Van Ryn (*left*), April 2007

◀ Sisters at Thanksgiving 2006: Laisa and Sandra, Carly and Whitney

▶ Friends from Taylor, May 2007: Whitney, Emily, Anne, Allie, Amy, Jen

Whitney's Father's Day card to
ewell, 2006

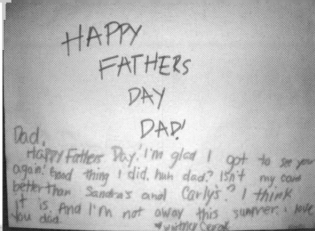

HAPPY
FATHERS
DAY
DAD!

Dad,
Happy Fathers Day. I'm glad I got to see you
again! Good thing I did, huh dad? Isn't my card
better than Sandra's and Carly's? I think
it is. And I'm not away this summer. I love
you dad.
♥Whitney Carol

Whitney with speech therapist from Spectrum
CC, Grand Rapids, 2007

▲ Whitney and Lisa leaving ICU hallway,
April 2007, "Retracing Our Steps"

◄ Whitney and Cindy Barrus, director of
operations, Spectrum CCC, Grand Rapids

◀ Five crosses on I-69 to represent lives lost on April 26, 2006: Laurel Erb, Brad Larson, Monica Felver, Betsy Smith, Laura Van Ryn

▲ Visiting Parkview Hospital, April 2007, Don, Sue, and Lisa Van Ryn; Whitney, Colleen, and Newell Cerak

▲ Taylor University Memorial Prayer Chapel

◀ Cerak family, Christmas 2006: Carly, Newell, Whitney, Colleen, Sandra fore I know she's ready. And I hate the idea of her being in that ambulance without one of us. This is the first time at least one of us hasn't been with her since the accident." She sighed. "I'll feel a lot better once we get there and get her settled into her room."

"She'll be fine. You'll see," he said.

"I guess so," she said. "But anything could happen, and there wouldn't be a thing they could do about it in that ambulance, away from the hospital." She looked over at Don as he drove the car. "I'm a mother. I can't help but worry about such things."

Don smiled. "I know."

The ambulance pulled into Spectrum Health Continuing Care Center a little after noon on Thursday. While the medical staff moved Laura into her room, Don and Susie filled out all the appropriate paperwork. Cindy Barrus, the center director, was waiting for them when they finished. "It's good to see you again," she said. Cindy had driven down to Fort Wayne to meet the family prior to the move, and they had discussed the particulars of the care Laura would receive at Spectrum. "Laura's quite a bit younger than our usual patients," she said as she led them down the hallway. "We specialize in working with patients with brain injuries, and the most common type of brain injury is a stroke, which usually occurs in older people. That's not to say we don't work with people Laura's age. We have another boy in here right now who's a little younger than Laura."

"Would you like to meet the people who will be working with your daughter?" she asked. Cindy led Don and Susie down another corridor and introduced them to the team of doctors and therapists who would take over Laura's care. "We have a lot of reading material here on brain injuries that you may find very helpful," Cindy added. She handed the books to Don, who took them for the family.

Eventually the family was allowed into Laura's room. Aryn wanted to be there, but he had gone back to work in Detroit the day before. Since Laura's accident, he had been working three days, then driving to the hospital to stay with her for three days. On the fourth day he had been returning to Detroit and repeating the process.

When the Van Ryns walked into Laura's room, they immediately noticed that her bed was different than the one they'd been shown prior to their arrival. After learning how active Laura had become, the staff had decided that she needed a bed that would provide her more protection.

"Wow," Lisa said, "looks like they're serious about keeping her from thrashing her way out of bed." The bed had a tall mesh side that zipped closed. Once the zipper was closed, Laura would not be in danger of rolling out of bed no matter how many scissor kicks she unleashed.

As the family moved closer to Laura, her face twisted up in pain.

"The trip had to be hard on her," Don said. "We should probably let her get some rest."

The Van Ryns stayed at the center a while longer before finally driving to their house in Caledonia. Susie hated leaving Laura, but the hospital assured the family that someone would be with her at all times. It was the only way Susie would agree to sleep at home that night, the first time the family had stayed in their own home since the accident three weeks earlier. "I'm not so sure how the place will look," Don said on the drive over. "Three weeks is a long time to be gone. The yard's probably out of control. Oh well, it's just grass. I'll get to it eventually."

When they pulled up to the house, they found the grass had been cut and the yard neatly trimmed. "Wow," Don said, "the place looks great. Someone even pulled the weeds out of the garden. Talk about going the extra mile."

The next-door neighbor pulled up in the driveway. He climbed out of his car and said, "Good to have you home. How's Laura?"

"Getting better every day," Don said. "You have any idea who's been mowing the yard? I would sure like to thank them."

"Pretty much everybody around here. We all took turns. We figured the last thing you needed to worry about was grass."

"I can't tell you how much I appreciate it. So many people have done so much for us over the past three weeks. It seemed like every day we were in Fort Wayne we got letters with gas cards and gift certificates to restaurants stuffed inside. And now this." He rubbed his head. "I've got to tell you, this is all very humbling. Thank you. Thank you so much."

"You'd do the same for me," the neighbor said. "Besides, I didn't want to have an overgrown lawn messing up the neighborhood," he joked.

As the Van Ryns walked into their home, a wave of emotion swept over them. The house was spotless, and the refrigerator and cabinets were stocked with food. A platter of freshly baked cookies sat on the counter.

Don and Susie walked into the living room and collapsed onto the sofa, and Susie began weeping. "I didn't realize how emotionally exhausted I was until right now," she said.

"It's good to be home," Don said. "We just needed to get home."

Two days later, Aryn arrived from Detroit. He walked into the Van Ryn home, breathed deeply, and smiled. "It smells like Laura here," he said. "I love it."

May 15, 2006

Burnout comes easy sometimes...especially working in the health-care field...seems recently I've depended on my own limited well of energy and emotion to get me through the daily grind. I want you, as a family, to know that through working with Laura, God truly has spoken to me and has renewed my passion for what I do.

I know, without a doubt, God has a purpose for Laura's life...and to see how He is awakening her is absolutely phenomenal. As we look to her moving on in her healing process and eventually leaving us here in Fort Wayne, I know, without a doubt, she will be in wonderful hands...but in a selfish way, a part of me will be sad.

Your family is a witness of Christ to the hospital staff and the buzz around the place regarding the love and patience that your family has is truly impacting the lives of us who have the awesome opportunity to work beside you.

"Hi"

Continue to wait on the Lord. His timing isn't always ours, as we know. But I trust and know that Laura is going to continue to make huge strides.

With all my love,

Joelle

Comment left on the blog

13

"LIFE WILL NEVER BE THE SAME AGAIN"

God is still a good God, and His promises are true. I will see Whit again. And these are not just things I say to get me by and to cope with my pain. I know the living God, and I will worship Him next to my sister again some day.

CARLY CERAK, SPOKEN AT THE MAY 7, 2006, TAYLOR UNIVERSITY
MEMORIAL SERVICE FOR ALL THE ACCIDENT VICTIMS

The last out-of-town relative had been ferried to the airport. The only cars left in the Ceraks' driveway belonged to Newell, Colleen, Carly, and Sandra. Between the graveside service and delivering the flowers from the funeral all over town, the previous day had been filled with activity. The family had taken most of the flowers to the Gaylord Intermediate School, where Colleen taught, and placed bouquets in front of each classroom door. As students walked in the next day, the school seemed to burst with color and the fragrance of all the flowers that had filled the church on the day of Whitney's funeral.

This was the first day that the house had been completely quiet since they'd returned to Gaylord and begun planning Whitney's funeral. The family had no more flowers to deliver, no more errands to run. Friends had backed away to give them their privacy. The clock struck eleven, but the basement was not filled with college students singing. Worn out from all they'd been through, Carly and Sandra had already gone to sleep.

Newell and Colleen crawled into bed, and although they were exhausted from the past several days, they didn't immediately fall asleep. They wrapped their arms around each other and lay in the dark listening to the silence. Finally Newell said, "She's really gone. Whit's gone and she's never coming back." His body began to shake and tears rolled down his cheeks. Colleen began sobbing as well. "This is it," Newell said. "This is the way life is going to be from now on. She's never going to come bursting through that door again, laughing. Her room will never be covered from floor to ceiling with clothes and everything else she owns. She is gone. Whit is really gone."

"How . . . ?" Colleen started to say. She stopped. Silence. Finally she said, "What do we do now? How does life ever go back to being normal? There is no more normal." She started to say something else, but the words wouldn't come out.

"I remember when we dropped Carly off at college the first time, when Whitney was only a junior in high school," Newell said. "As we pulled out of the Taylor parking lot, I heard her crying in the back seat. I asked her if she was going to be okay, and she said, 'Dad, life will never be the same.' I can hear her saying that just like she was right here in the room with us now. Life is never going to be the same."

"No, it's not," was all Colleen could say.

Sometime the next morning, Colleen, Carly, and Sandra made their way into Whitney's room. Carly and Sandra sat down on the bed, while Colleen moved around the room. She opened a dresser drawer and began pulling out soccer team shirts and School Spirit Week T-shirts. Then she moved to the closet and began thumbing through Whitney's clothes. The clothes smelled like Whitney, which made her seem very close, very alive. A bittersweet feeling.

"What are you going to do with everything?" Carly asked.

"I'm not sure," Colleen said. "I don't see much point in keeping all of it and making her room look like we're waiting for her to come back. But I don't want to just get rid of it."

"There are some of her clothes I would like to have, things that remind me of Whit," Carly said.

"Me too," said Sandra.

When Colleen told them to go through everything and take what they wanted, Carly said, "I wonder if any of Whitney's friends would like to have something of hers as well."

"That's a good idea," Colleen said. "After you two take what you want, I think I will invite Whit's friends to come by and take something that will help keep her memory alive for them."

"You're not going to give away her pictures and the things hanging here in her room, are you?" Carly asked.

"No, no, no. Not the pictures. Just her clothes," Colleen said. "I still want her room to look like her room. I don't want to change that. Not yet. Maybe not ever."

For the next couple of hours, the three of them went through Whitney's T-shirts and jeans and all of the clothes hanging in her closet. Once Carly and Sandra had taken what they wanted, they laid everything else out on the bed and started making phone calls. As girls began coming by the house, the most frequent question they asked was "Would it be all right if I take this? Whitney was wearing this when she and I . . ."

Hearing the stories from the girls reassured Colleen that she'd made the right choice. By the end of the day, all of Whitney's clothes had new homes. Colleen wouldn't have wanted it any other way.

When Newell opened the mail that afternoon, he found a note from a friend who'd attended Whitney's funeral. He tore open the envelope, expecting to find a note much like those that had poured in every day. Almost all of them expressed their deepest sympathy for the family's loss and pledged to pray for them in the days and weeks ahead. Newell put on his glasses, pulled the note from the envelope, and began reading. By the end of the second line he could hardly keep reading.

Dear Newell,

I wanted to send you a note of love and appreciation for all the special words of faith you shared with me today at Whitney's memorial service. God has truly blessed you. Whitney's life (and tragic death) was not in vain! Today during your heartfelt and inspirational walk through your daughter's life with you, I made a commitment to the Lord that I hope will change me and my relationship to Christ. You and your family are living your faith and have given me a tangible example of what Christian living is all about.

As a father, I know how hard it must have been to let your daughter go, but as a believer, I sensed your true joy in knowing that she is with God and in the perfect place He has chosen for her. God's peace at work! I pray that sometime in the future we can spend some time one on one, and share our common bond of faith. Mission accomplished!!

Sincerely, Rich

Newell pulled off his glasses and wiped his eyes. Tears flowed, but they were more tears of gratitude for the life Whitney had lived and the influence she still had than they were tears of sadness. *Thank you, Whit,* he thought. *You're still touching lives even though you're gone.*

He sat silently in the chair for quite some time, gently crying, thinking about his daughter. As he reflected on the life she'd lived, he began to think about the life she continued to live in the presence of God. *I wonder what Whit's doing right now. I wonder what she's experiencing, who she's met since she's been there, what she's thinking as she adjusts to life in heaven. "Adjusts" . . . I doubt if that's the right word, but I can't think of a better one.*

His thoughts turned to the day he and Colleen moved Whitney to Taylor and how nervous Whitney had been about leaving all her friends behind. *It didn't take her long to adjust to Taylor and fall in love with it. Did she go through anything like that last week when she went home to be with Jesus? What is her new home like? I've always known where Whitney was, and when something great happened to her, she would come home bubbling over and tell me about it. I wonder what she wants to tell me now about all the great things that have happened since she arrived in heaven?*

The more Newell thought about Whitney's new home, the more anxious he became to discover the answers. Throughout the visitation on the previous Saturday and during her funeral, he had told people over and over that he knew beyond a shadow of a doubt that Whitney was in the very presence of God in heaven. Now he wanted to know more. He wanted to know what heaven was like and what his little girl was experiencing there.

He got up, walked over to the table, and grabbed his Bible. Thumbing to the back, he looked up the word *heaven* in his Bible's concordance, which is a topical index of key words in the Bible. He read what Jesus said about heaven, and he read the description of it found in Revelation, the last book of the Bible. Still, he wanted more. Over the next several weeks he read several books about heaven, all written from an evangelical Christian perspective. The more he read, the more real the place became, and the more anxious he became to go there and join his daughter, singing praises to God.

Although the funeral had passed, the family had an additional service to attend. Taylor University had planned a memorial service for the five accident victims exactly one week after Whitney's funeral. Newell and Colleen dreaded the trip, not because of the memorial, but because Carly and Sandra would not return to Gaylord with them afterward. Both had decided to stay at home the week after the funeral to help Colleen and to mourn. But they still had two weeks of class left in the semester. Although she didn't want to, Carly knew she had to go back to Taylor. And Sandra needed to return to Grand Valley State. Both had put in too much work in the spring semester to walk away without finishing.

The Ceraks drove two cars down to Upland. Newell and Colleen rode in one, Carly and Sandra in the other. As they neared mile marker 66 on I-69, Newell looked over at Colleen. "Are you ready for this?" he asked.

"No. Are you?"

"No."

At mile marker 67 he slowed the car and pulled into the right-hand lane. A moment later he said, "I think that's it up ahead." He turned on the right-hand turn signal and eased the car over to the shoulder. Carly pulled in behind him. A couple of trucks zipped by, their wind shaking the car. Newell and Colleen looked at each other. Neither said a word, but both were thinking, *If just the wind from the truck shakes the car, can you imagine what it must have been like when . . .* Looking into the mirror on the driver's side, Newell said, "It's clear. We can get out now." Carly and Sandra got out of their car at the same time. The four of them quickly stepped off the asphalt highway shoulder and into the tall grass next to it. They joined arms and slowly walked over to the set of five crosses rising up from one support, which someone had placed at the site of the accident. The grass was still torn up in places, and the faint smell of diesel rose when the wind turned a certain way. They stared at the center median. The truck tracks were unmistakable. Cars whipped by. The sun was shining bright. No one said anything for several minutes. The four stood there, arm in arm, crying. Carly buried her head on her dad's shoulder. *Whitney died here,* Newell thought. He'd worked as an EMT when the family lived in Upland many years earlier. He'd responded to accidents on the interstate, and he could picture the scene of the crash in his head. He fought to push the images out of his mind.

"Let's pray," Newell said. "I know I need to."

He thanked God that this place wasn't the end. He thanked God for Whitney's life and for her faith. He prayed for the families of the other accident victims. But most of all, he prayed for God's grace and strength. The four of them needed it now more than ever.

After a few more minutes of silence, they walked back to their cars. As Newell turned the key, the CD in the car stereo began playing. On the way down he and Colleen had listened to the song "Come to Jesus" over and over. They played it again. The song became a prayer for both of them. *Oh God, we can't go forward without you.*

Taylor's president, Gene Habecker, hosted a dinner in his home for the families of the accident victims prior to the memorial service. While all of the families had been invited, only the students' families attended. As the Ceraks walked into the house, they were greeted by a Taylor staff member, who ushered them into the main room where the other families waited. The president said a few words, thanking the families for coming and expressing his and the university's deepest condolences. He then introduced each family. As he went around the room, Newell and Colleen looked into the eyes of each of the parents. *They know. They understand what we're going through. Others try. And they mean well. But the people in this room, they know what we're going through, because we're all going through it together.* Everyone in the room felt an immediate bond, as if they were all now a part of a club that none of them would have volunteered to join, and yet they drew strength simply from being with one another. The families mingled, shaking hands and introducing themselves. No one mentioned the accident except to say how sorry each of them was for the other, and that they were praying for one another. They didn't have to say anything more.

Shortly before the meal began, Wynn Lembright walked over to Newell and Colleen. He had been a good friend of the family for years. Ironically, he was one of the three university staff members who were asked by the hospital to match the names to the bodies immediately after the accident. "Newell, Colleen, I'm glad you came down for this. It means a lot to all of us here," he said.

"We appreciate you guys doing this for us. Everyone's prayers have meant the world to us," Colleen said.

Then Newell put his hand on Wynn's shoulder and said, "I can only imagine what you've gone through these past several days. I've been praying for you, that God would give you peace from the images of that night. This has had to be tough on you."

"I appreciate that very much," Wynn said. He gave Newell and Colleen both a hug, then went to speak to the other families.

Rediger Chapel filled to overflowing for the service. The Ceraks took their seats in the roped-off section reserved for the five families. As they walked in, Colleen could feel every eye on her. Looking around at the other four families, she knew they all felt the same way. She tried to get comfortable. "The last time I was here was for the prayer service the morning after," Colleen whispered to her husband.

Newell reached over and took her hand. "That's part of what's brought us this far," he said, "this family praying for us."

As part of the service, a friend or family member of each of the victims stood and spoke. A sense of pride welled up inside Newell and Colleen as Carly spoke. "Some of you may have missed the chance to know Whitney. She was only a freshman," Carly began. "When I think about how to describe her, the first word that comes to my mind is funny. She had the greatest sense of humor . . ." A grin broke out on Colleen's face. *That's the first word I would use too*, she thought. Carly concluded her short remembrance by saying, "It is when I draw near to God that I feel most near my sister, because I know she is in front of Him, worshipping at His feet. So I end with the encouragement of 2 Corinthians 4:17–18, "For our *light* and *momentary troubles* are achieving for us an eternal glory *that far outweighs* them all. So we fix our eyes not on what is seen, but on what is unseen. For what is seen is temporary, but what is unseen is eternal." *This is exactly what we want people to know,* Colleen thought, *this is the hope that's carrying us.* Tears ran down her face. As Carly walked down from the stage, Colleen gave her a hug, and they sat down together.

Newell hadn't planned on speaking at the memorial service. Saying all he had at Whitney's funeral had been difficult enough for him. But as he sat in the chapel, listening to the music, one song spoke to him. It spoke of what it means to follow Christ, and how following Him and making a difference in the world demands one's entire life, heart, soul, and strength. *That's it. That's what I want these people to know—that my daughter and all those who died in the crash all lived their lives for Christ with nothing held back.* Before he knew it, Newell found himself walking up on the platform and taking hold of the microphone. "I want to thank everyone in the Taylor family for your prayers and support. I know I speak for the other families when I say that we could not have made it through this trial without it. As I've sat and listened to everything that was said and done here today, I wanted to leave you with a challenge. And we just sang it. Following Christ demands your all. I want to challenge you to give it."

Because the Ceraks had lived in Upland for several years prior to moving to Gaylord, they had many friends in the area. A crowd gathered around them as they made their way out of Rediger after the service. As they moved through the crowd, Newell felt a hand across his shoulder. He looked up and the man next to him reached out and said, "Hi, Newell, I'm Don Van Ryn. I wanted to tell you how much I appreciated what you and your daughter said today. We're praying for you. I want you to know that."

Newell shook Don's hand. "Thank you, Don. That means a lot to me. I also want to tell you that we pray for Laura every day. We praise God that she survived the accident, and we're praying she gets better very soon. How is she doing?"

"She's improving. We can see progress every day," Don said. The two spoke for a few moments longer before Don dismissed himself so that he could go and speak to the other families. All of them expressed the same thoughts to him. The families of the accident victims were all pulling for Laura.

Later, Newell, Colleen, Carly, and Sandra gathered in one

room of their hotel, sat on the beds, and talked until three the next morning. When they first received news of Whitney's death, the four of them had been scattered from Michigan to Mississippi. In the week and a half since, they had hardly been apart. Sitting in the hotel room talking about Whitney, talking about what lay ahead in the coming weeks, they all knew that this would be their last time together for a while. Carly and Sandra had to go back to school. Newell and Colleen had to go back to work. Life refused to stand still, even though all four of them wondered how it could move on.

The family got up early the next morning, ate breakfast at a local restaurant, and then went to the Upland city park for one final time of prayer and to encourage each other with words from Scripture. "I don't want to stay. I want to go home with you," Carly said. "How am I supposed to walk back into my dorm knowing that Whitney should be in the opposite wing, but she's not? When I go to the dining commons, I know I will just find myself looking around for Whit before I realize she's not there. I don't know how I can do this."

"I know, Carly, I know," Newell said.

"I dread walking back into the house when we get home," Colleen said. "We had so many people in and out last week and so much to do. Now . . ."

"How are we supposed to just go on with life?" Carly asked. "How do Sandra and I just go back to class and take our stupid tests and work on our stupid papers and just keep on going like nothing happened? That doesn't seem fair."

"It's not," Newell said. He paused, then said, "Life won't ever be the same again. I don't know how we will ever get used to Whitney not being here. I can't imagine that this pain will ever diminish. All we can do is pray God carries us through it."

Later that day, after having said tearful good-byes to Carly and Sandra, Newell and Colleen walked back into their house. "This is it," Newell said.

"Yeah," Colleen said.

Their eyes met as they walked into the kitchen. They both broke down crying.

14

WAKING UP

Monday, May 22, 2006

We continue to be encouraged and impressed by Laura's fine motor skills. In physical therapy this morning she did well following commands—opening her eyes when they asked, sitting up on her own for short periods, moving her legs and arms, etc.

Let me take a minute here and try to answer a frequently asked question. "So, is Laura out of the coma now?" The answer to that is yes. However—is she alert, bright-eyed, and aware of all that's going on? No. As was stated above, her brain needs to be re-trained (or reminded, perhaps) to handle information. Once again, it's going to be a long road for her. This waking-up process is a slow one. And once again, we're reminded that God has spared her life for now. She is His. His beautiful child and we believe He's got something more for her on this earth. We're just blessed to be a part of her family and to have the opportunity to walk with her through this time.

BLOG ENTRY POSTED BY LISA VAN RYN

With one motion, Laura reached up, grabbed her neck brace, and tore it off, tossing it to the floor. "That's ten times today," Don said.

"How much longer are they going to keep that thing on her? She hates it," Susie said. She picked up the brace from the floor, walked over to Laura, who was sitting in her wheelchair, and put it back on her.

"The doctor said she has to wear it until she can tell him herself that her neck doesn't hurt. Even though the MRI didn't show anything, the staff wants to keep it on as a precaution. She's talking a lot more, but it may still be a while yet," Don reminded her.

Laura reached up and began pulling at the brace once more. Susie gently pulled her hand away from it. "Help me," Laura said.

"I wish I could. Oh, how I wish I could," Susie said. She sat back down and looked over at Don. "This is almost worse than when she was completely out."

"It will get better," he said.

"Home," Laura said very softly. "I want to go home."

Susie let out a long sigh. "I know she's mad at me for making her stay here."

"She doesn't understand what's going on. She's just awake enough to be uncomfortable and confused, but not enough to know why all of this is happening," Don said. "We just need to be patient. This is just a rough stretch."

As they talked, Kenny walked into the room. Susie turned to Laura and asked, "Laura, do you know who this is?"

"Kenny," she said.

"And do you know who Kenny is?" Susie asked.

"Brother," Laura said.

"That's right. Very good."

Aryn also walked into the room. "Who is this?" Susie asked.

"Aryn," Laura said. "Hi."

Aryn broke out in a smile. "That's a lot better than yesterday," he said. "While I sat with her she slapped me, pushed me away, hit me, and kicked me in the throat about five times. She was pretty active."

"Wow. That's crazy. Better you than me I guess," Don chuckled.

"Yeah, but she also told me she loved me, and that made it all worth it."

"Laura," Don said, "who gave you your Tiger's hat?"

She pointed toward Aryn.

"Good. Very good. She's getting a little more aware of things every day. Starting to recognize us a little better. It won't be long now," Don said.

Tuesday, May 23, 2006

Last night I sat with Laura while she was very restless. I was looking at her and thinking about how much I love her and am thankful for her. I did my best to protect her injured leg and arm and to keep her as comfortable as I could. She was really movin' and was wearing me out! I thought about how tired I was but that I would stay with her as long as she needed me to, no matter what. And then she started hitting me. And kicking me. She'd make a fist and swing it at me. She wanted me out of her way so she could do what she wanted to—which included ripping that neck brace off as quickly as possible. And then I thought, how many times have I done that same thing with God?

Blog entry posted by Lisa Van Ryn

"Can you tell me who these people are?" Don asked as he held up a photograph for Laura to see. She kept her eyes open much more now, although when she opened them, she opened them wide, as though she were staring through people rather than at them. A couple of days earlier Aryn had said he thought her eyes looked bluer than usual, but they still had that green tint he loved. However, the spark that danced in her eyes had not yet returned.

"Laurie, can you tell me who you see in the picture? Who is this right here?" Don asked as he leaned close to her and pointed to the first girl in the photograph.

"Courtney," Laura said. She had snapped the photograph of her four roommates during her junior year at Taylor.

"And who is this?"

"Sara."

"Good. Very good. And who is this?" Don asked as he pointed to the third girl.

"Brittany."

"Great. Great. And who is the last one here?"

"Ahhh, Teeny," Laura said, calling her friend Christine by her nickname.

"Very good. You got them all right," Don said. "Excellent."

Susie walked over to Laura and gently kissed her on the forehead. "I love you, Laura," she said.

"Love you," Laura replied.

By this point she appeared tired. The day had been filled with therapy, and it had taken its toll on her. As a nurse moved Laura from her chair to her bed, she threw off her neck brace. Susie retrieved the brace, and put it back on her. Laura became noticeably agitated. "I want my dad," she said.

Don walked over and sat beside her. She calmed down.

"Can I have a kiss?" Susie asked. Laura puckered her lips and Susie leaned down to kiss her. "I don't think she's holding any grudges," she said.

One night Don, Susie, Lisa, and Kenny went into the Spectrum cafeteria to eat a dinner brought to them by someone from their church. As they walked in, Mark was sitting at a table, cutting a bandanna into strips, which he then twisted together. "What are you doing?" Lisa asked.

"Making a necklace kind of thing," he replied.

"What for?" Lisa said.

"I had one already and I wanted some in different colors."

"Can I make one?" she said.

"Yeah. Go ahead," Mark said.

"I think we should all make one and wear them until Laura walks," Lisa said. Everyone in the family agreed. Walking was just one of the goals they had for Laura. They prayed that by the end of the summer she would be able to go with them to Upper Peninsula Bible Camp. The camp had been part of the Van Ryn family for generations, and through the years had become a special place for them. "Camp runs through the middle of August," Don said. "She'll make it up there by then. You'll see."

Wednesday, May 24, 2006

John 1:16: "From the fullness of his grace we have all received one blessing after another."

In therapy this morning she was doing some great things, including kicking a rubber ball with her right leg while she was sitting up. The ball was rolled toward her and she swung her leg at the right times to kick it back. She did the same with her hands hitting a balloon (a pink one) after it was tossed in her direction. This morning she also fed herself some applesauce, which she swallowed well and then washed down with a little bit of orange juice. I can't say it went quite as well this afternoon with the mashed potatoes, but I ducked at the right time and the wall and the shirt-sleeves have all been cleaned up. :-)

Blog entry posted by Lisa Van Ryn

"Laura, I want you to try to finish my sentences," said Laura's speech therapist, Stephanie. "They will all have one-word answers. Are you ready to try?"

Laura nodded.

"Okay, the sky is . . ."

"Blue."

"Apples are . . ."

"Green."

Stephanie smiled at Lisa, who attended most of Laura's therapy sessions. "She must like Granny Smiths," Stephanie said softly. "Laura, apples can also be another color."

"Red."

"You are doing really well. Now we're going to do something a little different. I will give you some words, and I want you to tell me the opposite. For example, I'll say 'black' and you'll say 'white.' Are you ready?"

"Yes."

"Black."

"White."

"In."

"Out."

"North."

"South."

"Very, very good. Laura, earlier today we talked about what day it is. Do you remember what today is?" Stephanie asked.

"Thursday."

"Excellent." Stephanie said. Turning to Don and Lisa, she said, "She is making a lot of progress. I've seen a marked change just in the week she's been here."

"That's what the physical therapist said too," Lisa said. "Laura sat up on her own for two minutes and played catch with a beach ball. She even lifted a cup up to her mouth and took a drink today."

"I'm not surprised. She really is making remarkable progress," Stephanie said.

Don took Laura back to her room, while Lisa stayed behind to talk to Stephanie a little more. "I think she's getting a little frustrated. She's trying to talk more, but she's not always very easy to understand. Her voice is still so soft, and she has trouble pronouncing all the words she's trying to use. And she also says things that don't make a lot of sense. So far she's called me Stephanie, April, and Carly, as well as Lisa."

"That's not unusual for someone with a traumatic brain injury," Stephanie said. "The neurons in her brain are looking for a place to land as they fire. The best way to think of what's going on in her brain is to see it as a file cabinet that's been turned over, and the contents of all the files have spilled out on the floor. Slowly but surely her brain is trying to put the papers back in the files and the files back in the right places. It will take some time. I know you've heard this a couple of dozen times already, but brain injuries like Laura's usually take about two years to heal completely."

"Do they always get the files back in the right places?" Lisa asked.

"No," Stephanie replied. "That's what's so encouraging about the progress Laura is making. Time is really the only way to tell how far a person will come back. Laura seems to be a real fighter, like she is determined to get back."

"That's my sister," Lisa said.

Friday, May 26, 2006

Laura slept for another five hours last night from two A.M. to seven A.M.—praise the Lord! She's had another pretty good day of therapy...enjoyed her Teddy Grahams and apple juice this afternoon. She also threw the Frisbee with Dad this morning—she was sitting up on the edge of a bed and gently throwing it a few feet to him. For occupational therapy, they've been encouraging her to write the past couple of days, and she's drawn a couple of recognizable shapes including an impressive star this morning. She does open her eyes quite a bit now, but it's tough to tell sometimes what she's focusing on.

Blog entry posted by Lisa Van Ryn

"Can you tell me what that sign says?" Aryn asked as he pushed Laura down the hall in her wheelchair. He loved pushing her around Spectrum.

Laura gazed at the large WARNING: ALARM WILL SOUND sign, her eyes wide and glassy, just as they had been since she first started opening them back in Fort Wayne. "Warning . . . alarm," she said.

"That's right, Laura. Good job," Aryn said. He stopped pushing the wheelchair and squatted down to where their eyes met. "I love you, Laura."

"I love you too."

"Can I kiss you?"

Laura puckered her lips and he kissed her softly. Aryn broke out in a smile. "I'm praying so hard for you. I miss you so much. I wish we could take off from here and go sit at Borders and just talk like we used to."

"Tell them I'm okay so they'll let me go home."

Aryn didn't know what to say. "I wish we could take you home. We'd do it in a heartbeat if we could."

Laura turned and appeared to pout. Later that evening she pushed him away when he came close to her. "What's wrong, Laurie? Did I do something wrong?"

"Annoying," Laura said.

"What? Am I annoying you?"

"Yes," Laura said. Then she swatted her hand at him, like she was trying to shoo a fly away.

By the next day, however, she was over whatever had annoyed her the day before. When Aryn walked into the room, Laura opened her arms for him to come over and hug her. "Kiss me," she said. Aryn was more than happy to oblige. "I love you, Hunter," she said.

"Hunter?" Aryn looked around the room at Don, Susie, and Lisa. "Did she just call me 'Hunter'?"

"Lie down beside me, Hunter. Lie down like a normal human." As Aryn lay beside Laura, she pulled him close to her. "Ask them if you can stay," she said.

"Hunter?" Aryn asked the rest of the Van Ryns.

"Don't worry about it," Don said. "She's been saying some really crazy things the past couple of days. She's called Lisa about four different names. But when Susie asks her who Lisa is, she says 'sister.' Stephanie even told us that yesterday she said her name was Whitney. Stephanie said she sees this sort of thing all the time with brain injuries, and that Laura's saying crazy things is a good sign. There's no telling what she may say before she comes out of this completely. Now if we can just keep her from tearing off her clothes all the time."

"She's doing that too?" Aryn asked.

"Yep," Don said. "Again, they tell us it's normal with a brain injury."

Sunday, May 28, 2006

Another great night of sleep for Laura last night. She slept from about 8:30 P.M. to 10:30 A.M. with a few stirrings in between. The nurse tells us that sleeping this much is a normal phase in the recovery process and we're glad she's made it to this point and is finally getting some rest! The sleep she's been getting over the past couple of days is especially encouraging because it appears to be the most "restful" sleep we've seen her get so far ... It also seems that Laura, over the past couple of days, is becoming more aware and alert. Yesterday when she woke from a deep sleep, she seemed a little more taken aback by her surroundings and wondered where she was. She has also said a few complete sentences and is getting better at letting us know what her needs are. We're hopeful that as her communication skills continue to improve; this will cut down on her frustration level as well.

Blog entry posted by Lisa Van Ryn

Sunday, May 28, 2006

Psalm 63:1–8. You had another restful night. I have so much to praise God for—even in the darkest moments of night, He is there. "My soul clings to you, your right hand upholds me." You are great, Laurie! You are starting to speak in small sentences—God is so good to us! They gave you a shower today and washed your hair with the "blonde shampoo" (your choice!). I tried to French braid [it] but gave up and did pigtails instead. You said it was okay.

Susie's prayer journal entry

I just think about how lucky I am to have dated you the past three years and to have gotten to know you so well. Every day it seems like little bits and pieces are coming back to you, which makes me really excited. I hate thinking about how I have to leave you tomorrow night. I wonder if you are going to have DV and me push you all around today. We went everywhere yesterday. My feet hurt so bad last night, but it was so worth it. I want to see you get better and I am willing to do whatever it takes. I really know what love is now. Sorry it took me so long to figure that out. You know I don't like to use that word flippantly, but Laura, I am not afraid to say it now because I really do mean it.

Letter from Aryn to Laura, Sunday, May 28, 2006

15

MISTAKEN IDENTITY

Monday, May 29, 2006

Ephesians 2:8–10: "For it is by grace you have been saved, through faith—and this not from yourselves, it is the gift of God—not by works, so that no one can boast. For we are God's workmanship, created in Christ Jesus to do good works, which God prepared in advance for us to do."

Laura slept through the night again and we're glad for that. Her clarity continues to improve. Earlier today she played a game of Connect 4 with the therapists and did quite well. While certain things seem to be coming back to her, she still has times where she'll say things that don't make much sense. Also, DV bought her a hat today that says "life is good."

BLOG ENTRY POSTED BY LISA VAN RYN

"Okay, Laura, I would like for you to write your name for me," the occupational therapist said. Even though it was Memorial Day, the hospital kept Laura on her regular therapy schedule. Already that day she'd played a game with one of the other therapists and made a good showing.

She seems like she's almost back to the surface from the deep water of this coma. Don smiled at the thought. *She's really coming back to us!* He went along with Laura through all of her therapies that day. Lisa had taken the day off to spend some time at a cousin's cottage at the lake. It was the longest she had been away from her sister since the accident.

Laura sat at a table in the therapy room, and Don stood back behind her just to one side. A couple of days earlier he'd stood in the same spot and tried sneaking a video camera in to record her progress. He didn't think she would be able to see him, but a noise made her turn her head, and he was caught. With a wave of her hand, she'd made it clear she didn't like having a camera in the room. Don immediately turned it off and never brought it back.

This time he stood back and watched as Laura, with a large sweeping motion, scribbled a word across the paper. She gripped the pencil with her fist, which reminded Don of the way she held it when she was a preschooler. As she wrote, her entire arm moved, as if it took all of her strength, and nearly all of her body's coordination, to move the pencil the way she wanted. Already during this session she'd attempted to draw a square and a triangle.

The therapist turned the paper around so she could read what Laura had written. "Are you sure this is your name?" she asked. Laura nodded her head. "Very good. Now, I would like for you to draw a circle for me."

After asking Laura to draw a few more shapes, the therapist said, "You did a really good job today. I'm proud of how hard you're working. We'll do some more writing tomorrow, okay?"

Laura nodded.

When Don walked over to thank the therapist for all she was doing, she handed him the paper on which Laura had written her name. "Take a look at this," she said. There scrawled across the page were the letters:

W-H-I-T-N-E-Y

"What in the world?" Don said, somewhat stunned. "What do you make of that? You know, Stephanie told us that Laura's said her name was Whitney a few times now during speech therapy. Why do you think she would do that?"

"It could be any number of reasons. Brain injuries can produce some very strange effects. Does she have a close friend named Whitney?"

"There was another girl in the accident named Whitney."

"It could be something as simple as Laura was sitting next to her when the accident happened. Or they may have spent some time together that night, and Laura's mind has fixated on that name."

"That's probably what it is," Don said. "It sure seems strange, though. But then again, she's been saying some really crazy things the past few days. She keeps calling her boyfriend Hunter. I don't think she even knows a Hunter."

"There you go," the therapist said. "Her neurons are firing, but they're landing in strange places."

As Don was wheeling Laura back to her room, she said something he couldn't quite make out. "What did you say, Laurie?" he asked. She said it again, but he still couldn't make it out. He stopped the wheelchair and leaned down close, his ear near her mouth. "Can you say it for me one more time?"

In a voice not much above a whisper, her lips barely open, she said, "False parents."

Don frowned as he finally understood the words. *False par-*

ents? You've said some crazy things the past few days, but this tops them all, he thought. He smiled at the irony of the statement. *False parents! Taking care of you for twenty-two years, forking out all that money for college, watching over you twenty-four seven while you've been in the hospital . . . I got your false parents right here!* He shook his head and laughed. "All right, Laurie, your false parent is going to take you to your room now." Although he didn't take the "false parent" statement to be anything more than another neural misfire, he decided not to say anything yet about this, or that Laura had written "Whitney" for her name. *No sense getting everyone worked up over nothing. I have to tell Susie as soon as I can. But not right now. Not with so many people around. I will do it later, when it's just the two of us.*

As Don turned into the door of the room, he found the boys there along with Aryn. Aryn seemed anxious to spend as much time as he could with Laura before he left to go back to Detroit that evening. He would be gone for another three days. "How about going for another walk?" Aryn asked.

"Okay," Laura said.

A short time after he had handed Laura off to Aryn, Don's cell phone rang. It was Lisa calling for an update. He stepped out of the room and walked down the hall to where he could be alone to talk to her.

"How did she do today?" Lisa asked.

"Pretty well. They had her play a game of Connect 4, and she nearly won. That would have been something, wouldn't it? It was cool to see her have a good time playing the game," Don said. Then he paused.

"What?" Lisa asked.

"Well, there's this one thing, and I haven't even had a chance to talk about it with your mom or brothers. You know, they've had her drawing all kinds of shapes, so today the therapist decided to try a word. Her name." He paused again to catch his breath. "And she wrote 'Whitney.' The therapist asked her if she was sure this was her name, and she nodded her head yes. She's told Stephanie the same thing a couple of times now. But to write it . . ." His voice trailed off.

"That's really weird," Lisa said. "Why do you think she did that?"

"I don't know. Her therapist said this is not unusual behavior for a brain injury patient, that it could just be something out of the blue, or that Whitney could have been the last person she talked to. One of the girls in the accident was named Whitney, right?"

"Yeah," Lisa said. "And I guess that could make sense, especially after all we've been hearing about brain injuries."

"I guess we should keep it low-key for now. What do you think?"

"Probably. By the way, I'm coming by Spectrum on my way home from here to spend a little time with Laura," Lisa said.

After hanging up the phone, Don joined Susie in the cafeteria for dinner. A couple of their friends, Jim and Mikki, had come over to spend the afternoon with them. About halfway through their meal, Aryn came by, pushing Laura in her wheelchair. "Aryn," Don called, "would you bring Laura over her for a minute? I want her to see somebody."

When Aryn pushed her over, Don said, "Laura, look who's here! Can you say hello to Jim and Mikki?"

"Hi."

"Hi, Laura," Jim said. He glanced over at Mikki and gave her a funny look.

"Hi, Laura, it's nice to see you again," Mikki said. The two were very quiet through the rest of dinner.

Don and Susie were still at Spectrum when Lisa arrived, but they seemed anxious to get home. Aryn had left a couple of hours earlier. "How was that?" Lisa asked her parents.

"Tough, as always," Susie said. "He loves her so much that he looks like he's in physical pain to leave her."

"I told your mom about the name thing," Don said.

"Did Laura say anything else strange today?" Lisa asked.

"The same stuff she's been saying. She keeps calling Aryn 'Hunter,' for whatever reason. That makes about as much sense as her saying her name is Whitney," Don said.

"I don't like this phase we're going through right now," Susie said. "I think in some ways it was easier to watch her when she was unconscious than to watch her struggle to get her thoughts together."

After her parents left to go home for the night, Lisa pulled a chair over close to her sister's bed and just looked at her. Laura had already been zipped into her bed and was trying to sleep. For the first time since the accident, something struck Lisa as odd. *I don't know what it is,* she thought, *but something about her just looks different. Something just doesn't seem right.* The thought left Lisa shaken.

A few minutes later she unzipped the bed, reached in, and gave her sister a kiss good night on the forehead. Throughout the drive home she felt nervous, jittery. She pulled up to the house and noticed all of the lights were out. Everyone else must have already gone to bed, she decided. She intended to go straight to bed herself; it was late and she wanted to get to Spectrum in time for Laura's first therapy session the next morning. *If it really is Laura.* The thought popped into Lisa's mind so quickly that it frightened her a little. *If it really is my sister.* As she turned the thought around and around in her head, she knew it had been growing there since her conversation over the phone with her father.

She turned on a light and walked through the kitchen. *I'm not sure the girl in the hospital bed is really Laura. What if it is Whitney?* She looked around the kitchen for a moment. *Whitney, Whitney. I know we have a CD around here that someone sent us with memories of Whitney.* Lisa began looking around the kitchen. She opened a few drawers and looked around the countertops before finding the CD on the snack bar. She looked closely at the picture of Whitney Cerak on the CD label. *That looks like her eyes! Those big eyes. I think I've been looking into Whitney's eyes for the past five weeks.* She turned the CD case over and saw a picture of Whitney smiling. *Those are her teeth!* Lisa's pulse raced as a feeling of dread swept over her.

Just then Don came walking around the corner. "Hey, Lis, when you go to bed, hit all the lights, okay?"

"How do we know it's really Laura in the hospital, Dad?" Lisa asked.

"What?" Don asked, taken aback by her question.

"How do we know this is really Laura? I know they called and told us Laura was in the hospital before we drove down to Fort Wayne. But who identified her? What kind of process did they use to make sure that it was really her?"

"Lisa, don't let her writing the wrong name shake you up. It already has your mom upset. She doesn't know what to make of all of this, and it has her worried. Think about it. Laura wrote the wrong name, but they told us that this is what brain injury patients do. After all, don't you think that if this wasn't Laura we would know it by now?" Don said. "We've been with her for five weeks!"

"You're probably right," Lisa said and gave her dad a big hug. "Thanks for the reassurance," she said as she went on upstairs to bed.

Memorial Day, 2006

Oh God—hear me. Please don't take Laura from me, Lord. My heart is heavy today. Please don't let it be. My heart cries out in desperation to you. I can only lean on you for strength. This would be more than I can bear. I know you are not a cruel God—what purposes would there be? Could my heart deceive me? Could I not know my own daughter? Oh God, help me. You are all I have. Please give me Laura back.

From Susie's prayer journal

Don and Lisa drove over to Spectrum together the next morning, but they didn't talk about their conversation from the night before. Lisa did her best to convince herself that she had no reason for doubt. Shortly after they arrived, Paul Johnston called and asked if he and Jim could come by that morning and talk with Don. Don told them to come around ten. When they arrived, he met them in the parking lot. A short while later, he returned alone. "What was that about?" Lisa asked.

"Yesterday while you were gone, Jim and Mikki came by here for supper. Apparently, when Aryn wheeled Laura over, they didn't think it looked at all like her. I guess thinking about this kept Jim up most of the night, so he talked with Paul about it, and they decided to come by this morning to talk to me. Jim kept asking me if I was sure it's Laura, because he doesn't think it is."

"What did you tell them?" Lisa tried to sound calm, but inside she panicked. A sick feeling hit her in the pit of her stomach.

"I said, 'Guys, don't you think I know my own daughter? Of course it's her.' But Jim was pretty insistent, so I told them I would do whatever it took to verify that it is Laura." The confrontation with his friends in the parking lot, along with his conversation with Lisa the night before, left Don with a numbness and a feeling he could not describe.

"I agree. We've got to do something to make sure. Have you talked to Mom about it yet?" Lisa said.

"No, but I guess I need to right away."

As Don and Lisa talked, Susie arrived at the center. She walked over to the two of them, anxiety scrawled across her face. "You're talking about whether this is Laura, aren't you?" she said.

"Jim and Paul came by. Jim said he didn't think the girl he saw yesterday was really Laura. Lisa and I have been talking about how we need to just make sure and figure out what's going on," Don said with a reassuring tone.

Susie felt her knees go weak. "What do you have in mind?"

"Do you know who identified everyone at the accident?" Lisa asked. "You could call them and talk to them."

"That's a good idea. Okay, Mom and I will go home and make some phone calls and try to figure all this out. I guess you should stay here. Laura has a therapy session coming up and one of us should be there."

Lisa agreed to stay. "Call me the second you know *anything*." As she watched her mom and dad get in their car, a wave of anxiety swept over her. "And please hurry," she called.

Lisa stood in the same spot for what felt like a very long time, unsure of what to do. *Too many questions, too many questions I don't want to think about. I know I need to go in and be with her for her next therapy session. I want to be with her, whoever she is.* Even if this girl was not Laura, Lisa had grown to love her. *I don't want her to think we've just abandoned her.* Lisa paced around the parking lot, her body shaking. *But who is she? If this isn't my sister, have we inflicted all kinds of emotional pain on her by calling her by the wrong name and acting like we're her family? Her family. If this is Whitney, she has to wonder why her family isn't here. I don't know what to do.*

Although she told her parents that she wouldn't talk this over with anyone else, Lisa called her friend Deb, who also happened to be a counselor. "I've got to tell you something, and I know it's going to sound unbelievable, but I just don't know what to do right now." Lisa poured out the short version of the story and heard an audible gasp when she got to the part where she thought Laura was actually someone else. Deb quickly regained control of herself and was able to calm Lisa down. She also told her that she needed to stay with "Laura" until all the questions were answered. Lisa thanked her friend, tried to regain her composure, and walked inside the center toward Laura's room. As she did, she called her parents but no one answered. *What is taking so long?* she wondered.

Laura's schedule for the day kicked off with physical therapy. The therapist took a beach ball, handed it to Laura, and said, "Throw the ball to your sister for me."

Lisa cringed inside. *That's not right. I might not be her sister. If I'm not, what must be going through her mind right now? How confusing does this have to be to her?* Outwardly, Lisa smiled and held out her arms. "Throw it to me," she said. Throughout the session, Lisa did not call the girl in the wheelchair by name. She couldn't bring herself to call her Laura. Whitney just didn't seem right yet either.

When Don and Susie arrived back at Spectrum, Lisa left the therapy session for just a moment to have a quick conversation with them. "Well?" she said.

"I talked to one of the people who helped identify the bodies at the accident." Don's voice trailed off.

"And?" Lisa asked.

Don let out a long sigh. "There's some room for doubt."

Lisa wanted to throw up. "Okay, what are we supposed to do now?"

"I'm not sure. We're going to go talk to the people here at Spectrum and ask them what the best way will be to make a positive identification of her," Don said. Susie remained quiet.

Her head spinning, Lisa went back over to the girl in the wheelchair as the therapy session wound down. She thanked the therapist, and pushed the girl out the door to go back to her room. As they went down the hall, Lisa took a detour to a secluded corner and stopped. She walked around to the front of the chair so that she could look the girl in the eye. Squatting down, Lisa said, "You did really well today. I'm very proud of you. You're working really hard to get better, and that makes me very happy."

"Thank you."

"Can I ask you a question?"

The girl nodded.

"Can you tell me your name?"

"Whitney."

"Yeah, that's right. That's really good. And can you tell me your parents' name?"

"Cerak."

Lisa could feel a lump building in her throat. "Is that your last name?"

"Yeah," the girl said in her soft whisper of a voice.

"Can you tell me your parents' first names?" Lisa's voice cracked just a little, but she fought off the tears.

"Newell and Colleen."

"Wow. That's great. You're doing awesome. I'm so proud of you," Lisa said. And in that moment, all of her doubts from the night before were confirmed. The girl they had been caring for these last five weeks was not her sister. Her reaction to this seemingly horrendous realization surprised her. It didn't feel like a painful knife in the heart. Instead, she knew how special this short conversation really was, and she chose to treasure it. Somehow she felt a connection to this girl. All of the strange things Whitney had said over the past few days now made sense. Lisa pushed her down the hall to her room. A few minutes later a nurse came and took her to her next therapy session. Lisa went to find her parents.

"She told me her name was Whitney Cerak," Lisa said. She could barely keep from hyperventilating as she spoke, "and she said her parents' names are Newell and Colleen."

Don felt himself go completely numb. "That pretty much seals it, doesn't it?" he said. "There's no way Laura would know that." Susie grabbed his arm and began to weep.

"That's what I thought too. So what's the next step?" Lisa said.

"We need to talk to Cindy Barrus and confirm this and get the right parents here as soon as we can," Don said.

"I can't believe this is happening," Susie said. "I just can *not* believe it."

Don and Susie went directly to Cindy's office, which was located next to one of the therapy rooms, while Lisa waited on a bench in the hallway. As Don and Susie approached Cindy's door, they walked right past "Laura" working with a therapist on the parallel bars. "Laura," the therapist said, "that was great! Can you show your parents what you just did?"

Don and Susie heard "Laura" mumble, "They're not mine."

She's right, Don thought to himself, *I think she's so right, bless her heart.*

They knocked on Cindy's door and walked in. Cindy stood up next to her desk, "Don and Susie, it's good to see you. What can I do for you?" she said.

"Cindy," Don said softly, "we don't think this girl is really Laura."

Cindy gasped, sat down in her chair, and put her hand on her chest.

"Lots of things have come together to make us pretty sure she's not. I think we need to do something to positively identify this girl. We were thinking maybe fingerprints or something," Don said.

The color drained from Cindy's face. "Yes, let's see if we can do that."

"Earlier at home we found Laura's birth certificate, but it has only her footprint on it," Don said.

"That's a problem," Cindy stammered. Her mind could not catch up with what she'd just been told.

"What about dental records? Would those work?" Don asked.

"Absolutely," Cindy said. "I know a forensic dentist who would probably be able to do this for you."

All three of them glanced over at the clock. "It's nearly five," Don said. "If we're going to do this, we probably need to get on it right away. Do you have a phone book? I don't know our family dentist's phone number by heart."

"Yes, sure." Cindy handed the book across the desk to Don. He called his dentist, who assured him that he would take care of everything.

A few minutes later, Don and Susie walked out of Cindy's office to head home. Cindy had promised to call them there the moment the dentist's report was in. "Should we stop by her room to see her?" Don asked. Even as he said it, they both knew the answer. Both were convinced that the dental check would confirm what they already knew to be true. All of the strange behavior, all of the small changes that they'd passed off as a result of the accident, started to replay in their minds. As they walked down the hall toward the main entrance, Susie gripped Don's hand tightly. "When I saw her, in that therapy room . . ." Her voice cracked. She swallowed hard, tears streaming down her face. "When I saw her there, she still looked like Laura to me."

"Me too, Suz," Don said. "Me too."

Am I being tested, God? Let me come out victorious in your strength. Help me to focus on your ways day and night and rest on the knowledge that you alone are in control. You hear my prayers, you know my desires, Lord. Fill me with peace that I will be content with your outcome. Lord, I know that you are not a cruel God. I am fighting against those negative feelings. You are always with me.

How much can I bear? Only you know. Lord, lift me up today.

"Praise our God, O peoples, let the sound of his praise be heard; He has preserved our lives and kept our feet from slipping. For you, O God, tested us, you refined us like silver. You brought us into prison and laid burdens on our back. You let men ride over our heads; we went through fire and water, but you brought us to a place of abundance" *(Psalm 66:8–12).*

Today, God, I will rest in you.

From Susie's prayer journal, Tuesday, May 30, 2006

16

TELLING THE FAMILY

"Praise be to the God and Father of our Lord Jesus Christ! In his great mercy he has given us new birth into a living hope through the resurrection of Jesus Christ from the dead, and into an inheritance that can never perish, spoil or fade—kept in heaven for you, who through faith are shielded by God's power until the coming of the salvation that is ready to be revealed in the last time. In this you greatly rejoice, though now for a little while you may have had to suffer grief in all kinds of trials. These have come so that your faith— of greater worth than gold, which perishes even though refined by fire—may be proved genuine and may result in praise, glory and honor when Jesus Christ is revealed. <u>Though you have not seen him, you love him: and even though you do not see him now, you believe in him and are filled with an inexpressible and glorious joy.</u> for you are receiving the goal of your faith, the salvation of your souls" (1 Peter 1:3–9).

VERSE 8, UNDERLINED ABOVE, WAS
LAURA'S FAVORITE VERSE IN THE BIBLE

Every night since they'd returned from Fort Wayne, the Van Ryn family had eaten dinner together in the Spectrum cafeteria. Most nights someone from their church or another friend brought a meal to them, and they ate it there together.

Not this night.

Don called both of his sons and told them the family was going to have dinner at home. Neither Kenny nor Mark asked why, which left Don relieved. He didn't want to give them the impression that something was wrong, and he certainly didn't want to tell them this news over the phone.

Soon after he, Susie, and Lisa arrived home, Susie asked, "Shouldn't you call Mike and ask him to bring the food here rather than to the center?" Mike DeVries and his family were scheduled to bring dinner that evening. Longtime friends of the Van Ryns, they had looked forward to spending time with Laura for the first time since the family had returned to Grand Rapids.

"You're right, I almost forgot," Don said. He called Mike and asked him to bring the food to their house rather than to Spectrum. When Mike asked why, Don could not force the reason out of his mouth. "Something's happened." He paused for a moment to gather his thoughts. "We're pretty sure that . . . uh . . . this hasn't been Laura that we've been taking care of."

Don could hear the shock in his friend's voice through the phone. When Mike asked if there was anything he could do for them, Don asked, "Could you bring the food over yourself tonight, alone, and stay for a while? I would appreciate your being with us right now, if you don't mind." Mike immediately said he would be there.

Don glanced at his watch after hanging up the phone. He sat in a chair on one side of the room; Susie sat near him on the sofa, and Lisa sat across the room in a rocking chair. "So how do we want to do this?" Lisa asked. All three of them fought their emotions. The past two days had been extremely intense as the mystery of the identity of the girl in the hospital unraveled before them, a mystery none of them had known existed. The girl they believed to be Laura was actually Whitney Cerak. And that meant . . . None of them could give voice to the horror that they now knew to be true, not until the entire family was together.

Susie said very quietly, "I don't think any of us *wants* to do this." She sighed. "I wish it didn't have to be done." Sitting in the living room with Don and Lisa, waiting to break this horrific news to her sons, reminded her of another day five years earlier. On that day they had had to tell Mark and Kenny that Matt Van Ryn, their twenty-year-old cousin, and a girl named Mylissa, one of their closest friends, had been killed in a similar accident. Their car had been struck by a truck not far from the Upper Pennisula Bible Camp. Susie didn't want to watch her sons go through that pain again.

"I don't know if we can really even plan how to break the news to them, other than to just do it," Don said. His eyes were red and swollen. He paused, regained his composure, and prayed silently, *God, help me. Give me the right words to say when I break this news to my boys.*

Mike arrived a short time later, food in hand. He hugged Don and told him how sorry he was for his loss. Susie and Lisa walked over toward the kitchen, and Mike hugged them as well, tears flowing freely. The boys arrived home soon after. "Hey, guys," Don said, "can you come into the living room? We need to talk about something." Kenny and Mark walked in, puzzled looks on their faces. They looked around the room at Susie and Lisa and could tell something was wrong.

"What's going on?" Kenny asked. "Did something happen with Laura?"

"Have a seat, guys. That's what we need to talk about," Don said.

"What? What's going on?" Mark asked.

Don searched for the words. "We found out tonight that the girl in the hospital isn't Laura. Laura died in the accident with Brad and the other kids."

As the words left his mouth, the weight of what this news truly meant hit the entire family. Tears erupted along with shouts of "Noooo, that's impossible!"

Don took a deep breath, fought to hold himself together, then continued. "You know we wouldn't tell you this if we weren't sure it was true. They're doing a dental check right now to confirm it. They will call us with the results, but we already know what the answer is." He went on to explain as best he could everything that had happened over the past two days.

"*No, no, no,* I know it's Laura. I know it's her. I know my own sister! How could this happen?" Mark said.

"I'm so sorry." Don's voice broke as he said the words. "Laura didn't survive the accident."

The family fell into one another's arms. Susie ached, not only for the loss of her daughter, but for the pain her children now felt. All of the pent-up emotion of the previous five weeks, all of the fears of the worst-case scenario coming true came flooding out as reality set in. Along with Brad Larson, Betsy Smith, Laurel Erb, and Monica Felver, Laura Van Ryn, not Whitney Cerak, had died on April 26.

Overcome with emotion. Don fell to his knees on the floor, sobbing. "I'm going to need all of you so much through this," he cried out to his family. "We're all going to need one another." They all embraced and wept together on the floor.

Again Mark and Kenny wanted to know, "How could this happen, Dad? Is there a chance the dental records could prove you're wrong, and that it really is Laura?"

"No. I don't think so."

"I can't believe it until we hear back from the dentist. I can't believe she isn't Laura," Mark said.

"I know, son. I know," Don said.

The boys peppered Don, Susie, and Lisa with more questions. After a while, they calmed down, and everyone ended up in the kitchen. Mike asked, "Do any of you want some of the food I've brought?" Don could tell from his tone of voice that Mike hated to ask. No one felt like eating.

"Thank you so much for being here, Mike," Don said. After more tearful hugs, Mike said a prayer for the family and excused himself.

The Van Ryns settled back into the living room and waited for the call from Spectrum with the dentist's report. "I can't take just sitting here," Lisa said. "Let's go outside and shoot some baskets." Everyone agreed. She and her brothers got a game of Horse going, while Don and Susie sat on the porch swing and watched. After a few games of Horse, the family decided to take a walk down their long, private driveway. As they were walking, Don said, "I could use some ice cream."

"Me too" was the general consensus. Everyone got in the car and headed out to the local dairy bar. As they sat eating their ice cream, Lisa thought, *I needed this. I needed to do something normal, something we always do as a family. I needed to shoot baskets. I needed to come here.* She let out a long sigh. It had been a very long five weeks. "Hey, Mark," Lisa said to her brother, "do you remember when we were little how Laura used to order the exact same thing as you when we would go out to eat, just to drive you crazy?" They laughed.

"That was probably the only mean thing she ever did in her life," Susie said. "That girl didn't have a mean bone in her body. She was always so cheerful, so happy."

"Oh, she could make me laugh," Lisa said. "She used to say some of the craziest 'blonde' things." The more the family talked, the more it felt as if Laura were right there with them. It was a good feeling.

"Yeah, but she never said anything bad about anybody. Ever," Don said. *I'm going to miss her so much!*

When they returned home, Don went out into the front yard with his cell phone and dialed Aryn's home in Detroit. He dreaded making this call. Aryn's father, Jim, answered. He'd dropped by Aryn's house to do some painting. Just like the night of the accident, Aryn wasn't home. "I've got something to tell you, and you better get down off the ladder." Don paused, then continued, "There's been a mistake. The girl in the hospital isn't Laura. Laura died in the accident."

Jim could not believe what he was hearing. He began weeping loudly and asked how this could possibly be true. Both Jim and Trixie had visited the hospital many times over the past five weeks. They were very close to Laura and had already started thinking of her as a daughter-in-law. Still in disbelief, Jim said he would track Aryn down right away.

Aryn called Don back within an hour. When he did, his voice broke, the words would barely come out. "No, no, no," he said, "it's Laura. I know it's Laura. If anyone would know who she is, it would be me."

"I'm sorry," Don said as he struggled to hold back the tears. "We can hardly believe it ourselves, but it's true. We are waiting to get the report back from the forensic dentist, but we already pretty much know this isn't Laura."

"No, no, no. There is no way this is true. There is no way that's not Laura."

"Aryn, I'm so sorry. I wish this wasn't true. I cannot tell you how much I wish this wasn't true." Through their tears, the two talked for a short while longer. It was the hardest phone call Don had ever made.

He hung up and walked back inside the house. A few minutes later the phone rang again. It was Cindy from Spectrum. "Don," she said. "I'm very, very sorry. Laura's dental records did not match. It isn't her."

"Thanks, Cindy. We already knew that's what they would find. That means the girl in the bed has to be Whitney Cerak," he said.

"Probably, yes. We'll make sure . . ." She stammered for a moment. "I'm really, really sorry to have to break the news to you like this."

"That's okay. Thanks again for taking care of everything." He hung up the phone, and turned to the rest of the family. Very quietly he said, "Cindy said the dentist confirmed that it is not Laura."

Another wave of raw emotion swept over them, even though they had fully expected this outcome.

As she climbed into bed, later that night, Lisa thought, *I wonder how Whitney is doing?* For five weeks she and her family had loved and cared for this girl. Discovering she wasn't who they thought she was did not change the fact that they wanted her to get out of that bed and make a complete recovery. As Lisa thought about Whitney, she prayed for her, just as she had every day for the past five weeks.

The only difference was the name she used for the girl she'd thought was her sister.

Wednesday, May 31, 2006, 1:00 P.M.

"Jesus Christ is the same yesterday and today and forever." What may come to us as a shock does not shock the One who made us. We have some hard news to share with you today. Our hearts are aching as we have learned that the young woman we have been taking care of over the past five weeks has not been our dear Laura, but instead a fellow Taylor student of hers, Whitney Cerak. There was a misidentification made at the time of the accident, and it is uncanny the resemblance that these two women share. Their body types are similar, their hair color and texture, their facial features, etc. Over the past couple of days, as Whitney has been becoming more aware of her surroundings, she has been saying and doing some things that made us question whether or not she was Laura. Yesterday, we talked with a Spectrum staff member and began the process of making a positive ID. We now know without a doubt that this is Whitney.

The Cerak family came down from Gaylord, and we had the privilege of meeting with them this morning. While we discussed some of the action steps that will need to take place over the next couple of days, we were also able to share with them some of the great things we have seen Whitney accomplish over the past month. It is a sorrow and a joy for us to learn of this turn of events. For us, we will mourn Laura's going home and will greatly miss her compassionate heart and sweetness, while knowing that she is safe and with her King forever. We rejoice with the Ceraks, that they will have more time on this earth with their daughter, sister, loved one. We also want to thank you for your prayers for our family as well as the other families during the past few weeks. Your love and support have been amazing. It is our hope that the Ceraks would continue this blog in Whitney's name so that we may continue to pray with them for Whitney as she recovers. Please continue to check this site, and we will let you know about this possibility. We will also use this site to communicate our plans for a memorial service for Laura. Hopefully, this service will take place this coming Sunday. Thanks again for the support that you've been. Please continue your prayers. Our God is good and continues to be our help, our guide, our comfort.

We love you, Sweets.

Blog entry posted by Lisa Van Ryn

Wednesday, May 31, 2006, 3:15 P.M.

Laura's Memorial Service is scheduled for 3:00 P.M., Sunday, June 4. There will be a reception following. It will be held at Kentwood Community Church.

Blog entry posted by Lisa Van Ryn

Laura Jean Van Ryn,

This will be my last letter to you. For the past 35 days my heart and mind have gone through more than any man should ever have to go through. I am sorry, Laura, that I didn't know it wasn't you. I feel like I am the one who should have known. Laura, I have cried and mourned so much for you. You were an amazing woman that won my heart like nobody has done before. I really looked forward to being with you again. It is hard for me to think what day marks the end of our relationship. April 26, the worst day of my life and May 30, the day I ended the relationship. My heart will always love you. I didn't have enough time with you here on Earth. Where do I go from here? . . .

From Aryn's last letter to Laura. He wrote to her at least once every day during the five weeks of "Laura's" coma.

17

BACK FROM THE DEAD

Thursday, June 1, 2006

"By faith Abraham, when God tested him, offered Isaac as a sacrifice...Abraham reasoned that God could raise the dead, and figuratively speaking, he did receive Isaac back from death" (Hebrews 11:17, 19).

I couldn't get this verse out of my head as we drove down to Grand Rapids. I did not believe my sister was in the hospital; I thought for sure this was a mistake. When I walked into the hospital room, I was shocked and overcome with joy.

Soon after we saw Whitney, our family met with the Van Ryns, and our joy for ourselves was pushed aside by the pain we felt for them. It is hard because our joy is their pain. The Van Ryns have been amazing to Whitney, and we are privileged that, if under any care besides ours, she was under their great care. However, we know the pain they now feel all too well and our hearts break with them. There is a deep connection that has been made between our families, and together we look to God as we walk through this.

[Whitney] began listing people she wanted to see, starting with our dad [who was on his way back from New York with the youth group]. She kept telling us to call him, and when she talked to him, she told him she loved him and to "come over."

BLOG ENTRY POSTED BY CARLY CERAK

Newell hung up the phone in stunned disbelief. Colleen had just called from Whitney's bedside, confirming that the daughter they had thought was dead was actually alive. He sat down, rubbed his hand through his hair, and said to himself, "I've got to get home. I have got to get home to Whitney. *Now!*" he blurted out to no one. "And I've got to tell somebody about this!"

Newell had taken a group of high school seniors to a church in New Jersey, forty miles outside of Manhattan. His sister, Joan, and her husband pastored the church. Joan and her family were already awake when Newell banged on her apartment door a few minutes before seven. She opened the door and stared at Newell with a puzzled look on her face.

"I need to talk to you," he said as he motioned for her to come outside.

"What's wrong?" she said. "You look like you've seen a ghost."

"I don't know how to tell you this, but I just got off the phone with Colleen and, Joan, Whitney is alive." The look on his sister's face told Newell that she thought he really had seen a ghost. He could read in her eyes that she had no idea what he was talking about. "No, no, no, you don't understand. The people who identified the bodies at the accident scene made a mistake. The girl we buried wasn't Whitney. She's alive right now in a hospital in Grand Rapids," he said.

Joan let out a shriek and fell to the ground. "I can't believe it!"

Newell knelt down next to her and wrapped his arms around her. They hugged for a long time. Joan's husband, Andrew, walked out of their apartment and said, "What's going on?" When Newell gave him the news, his reaction was the same as Joan's. Once

Newell finally convinced his brother-in-law that Whitney really was alive, he said, "I hope you guys don't mind, but I think we're going to take off a little early." The trip was supposed to last one more day.

"Are you kidding?!" Joan said, "Get out of here. Go!" Unable to contain her joy, she shouted, "Whitney is alive. Hallelujah. She's alive!" As he left, Newell asked her to start calling everyone in the family to give them the news. Of course she was ecstatic to do it.

Newell walked back to the dorm rooms where his students were sleeping. Glancing at his watch, he saw it was only seven-thirty. They had arrived back on campus after midnight the night before, and no one had gone to sleep before one. *They can sleep on the bus,* he thought to himself as he rushed over to the girls' side and announced, "Everybody needs to get out of bed right away and meet me at the table in the middle of the campus. I have to talk to you about something." He did the same thing on the boy's side. As the kids came stumbling out of their dorms, they began asking, "What's wrong? What did we do? Are we in trouble?" Once they were all gathered around, Newell said, "I just received news that there was a mistaken identity on the night of Whitney's accident. She did not die. She is alive."

Shocked silence filled the air. Finally, someone yelled, "What?"

"I said, there was a mistake in identifying the victims on the night of Whitney's accident. She did not die. She is alive and right now she's in a hospital in Grand Rapids, asking for me."

"Let's go!" came a shout. Some of the kids cried softly. Others stood back, huge grins on their faces. Soon everyone was crying and embracing one another.

"So if it's okay with all of you, I'm going to cut our trip short by a day," Newell said with a big smile. The group agreed and ran back to their cabins. Within half an hour their bus was packed, loaded, and on the road with Newell behind the wheel, the gas pedal pinned to the floor. He couldn't get home fast enough.

Back in Grand Rapids, the Van Ryns drove over to Spectrum Hospital. Cindy Barrus had arranged for the two families to meet each other at eight in the morning. "Let's all ride in my car," Don said. He and Susie climbed in the front, while Lisa, Mark, and Kenny rode in back. As she settled into her seat, Lisa looked around. *We can all fit in one car now,* she thought. *Now there's only five of us, and we can all take one car.* She shook her head and recoiled at the thought.

Cindy greeted the Van Ryns at the door and ushered them into a conference room. "Are they here?" Susie asked.

"Yes, they got in just a little while ago. They're back with Whitney right now," Cindy said. Susie saw tears well up in Cindy's eyes.

The Van Ryns walked into the conference room and shook hands with the assistant coroner and sheriff's deputy from Grant County, Indiana. Don pulled the two officials out into the hall and asked, "So how did this happen? How could a mistake like this be made?" His tone was not accusatory. He simply wanted to know the process they had used to identify the accident victims, and how Whitney had been misidentified as Laura.

"Well, Mr. Van Ryn, in a large accident like this . . . ," one of them began.

The two men struck Don as nice guys, but their answers were guarded. All he wanted was an explanation. "I'm not here to lay blame on anybody. I'm just trying to understand what happened."

The two then explained how in the chaos of the accident scene, the rescue workers had found Laura's purse next to a blonde-headed girl who looked enough like the picture on the driver's license in the purse to allow them to assume she was Laura. Later, three officials from Taylor confirmed the identities of all the victims. "Were any of the families ever asked to make a positive ID?" Don asked. The two could not answer one way or another.

The three talked for a few moments more. Don thanked them and rejoined his family in the conference room. He sat down next to Susie, who appeared visibly shaken. "Are you okay?" he asked.

"I hope they don't resent how long we went without realizing this was Whitney. I can't imagine what's going through their minds. They must think we were clinging to her out of some false hope. I'm afraid they might think we were trying to keep their daughter from them," she said.

Before Don could answer, Colleen, Carly, and Sandra walked into the room, with Jim Mathis trailing behind. Susie walked over and hugged Colleen. Instantly Susie's fears evaporated. She whispered in Colleen's ear, "I am so happy for you." Her words made Colleen burst into tears and she hugged Susie harder. "We know how you feel, and we are so excited for you that you have your daughter back," Susie said.

Colleen pulled back and looked Susie in the eye. "I want to tell you how much our hearts break for you." Susie knew that Colleen understood exactly what she was going through.

Lisa walked over and hugged Carly, then Sandra. Before the Ceraks walked into the room, Lisa had felt a combination of anxiety and excitement. Like her mother, she was a little worried about how the Ceraks would view them. However, she was more excited to tell them about how far Whitney had progressed over the past five weeks and to bring them up to date on her condition. There were hugs all around. The families soon discovered another connection. Jim Mathis had led a team of volunteers on a mission trip to the Dominican Republic several months earlier. Mark Van Ryn had been part of that group.

Once the hugs and tears subsided, the two families sat down at the table across from each other. Don spoke first. "I know you guys must think we are the world's biggest dopes for not knowing our own daughter. It's a really long story, and I guess eventually we'll probably have a chance to tell you the whole thing, but for now, I just want to assure you that we were told Whitney was Laura, and we never had a reason to doubt it. But the second we figured this out, we wanted to get you here. We're sorry it took so long."

"Please, please, there's no need to apologize. We are so appreciative of all you did for Whitney over these five weeks," Colleen said.

"She's come a long way. We're just happy that she's finally

back with her real family. The last thing we wanted to do was confuse her or deter her progress. We hope we haven't screwed things up in her mind. But more than anything, we're happy for you that you have your daughter back," Don said.

Colleen touched her hand to her chest. The fact that the Van Ryns could be happy for her while grieving their own loss touched her deeply. She swallowed hard and said, "Thank you. And thank you for loving our daughter as your own for these five weeks. I also want to tell you how sorry we are for your loss. We know the pain you feel. I am so sorry that you have to go through this."

Don thanked them. Deep inside he'd already accepted that Laura had died on April 26. He didn't feel angry at God for taking her away. *Parents have to bury their children every day. Why would I assume that God would feel obligated to keep that from happening to us?* he'd thought to himself over and over during the past twenty-four hours. And when he told the Ceraks he was happy for them, he meant it. He knew how it felt to have your child survive an accident in which she probably should have died. He understood the joy they now felt, and he and the rest of the family genuinely shared it with them.

"We probably don't have time to get you up to date on her medical stuff, and I assume the staff will do that anyway. However, I can tell you that she hates her neck brace. One day I think she tore it off fifteen times," Don said. Everyone in the room laughed.

As the conversation went on, a nurse walked into the room and took Colleen by the arm. "She's asking for you, Mom."

Colleen smiled, jumped up, and said, "I'm sorry, I have to go." Carly and Sandra followed right behind her.

Susie let out a gasp of excitement. *That's the moment I was looking forward to for these five weeks. That moment when she would finally recognize me.* Reaching over, she took hold of Don's hand. A tear ran down her cheek as she told him, "This is right. This is how it should be. I am so thankful that when she could finally ask for her mother, her mother was here for her."

SPECTRUM HEALTH

For Immediate Release Contact: Bruce Rossman

The Families of Laura Van Ryn and Whitney Cerak Stand Together in Issuing This Media Statement

We are experiencing a wide range of emotions upon learning that the young woman being cared for at the Spectrum Health Continuing Center is Whitney Cerak and not Laura Van Ryn. These two wonderful young women shared a striking similarity in size, hair, facial features and body type.

As Whitney continued to heal from her injuries and became more conscious of her surroundings, her comments led the Van Ryns to doubt that she was their daughter Laura. The Van Ryns brought their concerns to Continuing Care staff, who initiated an exam of dental records. By late Tuesday evening it was determined that Laura's dental records did not match those of the patient at the Continuing Care Center. Whitney's identity was confirmed through her dental records early Wednesday morning.

In addition to sharing a striking similarity in appearance, Laura, Whitney and their families share a strong faith in Jesus Christ and are united together in His love. Our families are supporting each other in prayer, and we thank our families, friends and communities for their prayers. We are going through an emotionally difficult time and ask that everyone please respect our need for privacy.

Press release issued by both families through Spectrum, June 1, 2006

The church bus struggled to maintain its speed going up the Pennsylvania hills on I-80, but Newell never let up on the accelerator. He made up for the time going up hills on the way back down. The motor whined and the temperature gauge crept higher and higher. Newell didn't notice, and he didn't let up on the gas. After several hours of driving after a night without sleep, he allowed one of the other men to drive. He went to the back of the bus to try to get some rest. He turned his cell phone on, and it immediately started ringing. "Dad," the voice on the other end said.

"Hey, Carly, how are things going there?"

"Pretty good. I have someone here who wants to say something to you." Carly handed off the phone, and a soft, almost whisper of a voice came on the line. "Hi, Dad. I miss you. Hurry back," Whitney said.

Newell could hardly keep himself together long enough to say, "I'm on my way, Whit, I'm on my way."

He hung up the phone and closed his eyes. The phone rang again. Colleen's brother called. Then Newell's brother. Then more family. Once more it rang, but Newell didn't recognize the incoming number.

"Hi, Newell Cerak. This is Diane Sawyer's producer from ABC News." It was the first of many, many calls he received from different media outlets. Finally he asked the producer from the *Today* show how the person had gotten his number, and was told, "Mr. Frank, who I believe is your father-in-law, gave it to us." Newell immediately called Colleen, and together they figured out that the news crews had found her parents' names through Whitney's funeral announcements. When the media called, her father had been so excited about Whitney being alive that he wanted to talk to anyone who asked about it. He gave out Newell's cell phone number without realizing who had asked for it. Newell's phone continued to ring during the bus ride home. He was never able to get any sleep.

Not long after Newell handed over the driving responsibilities, the bus slowed down for a construction zone. Two lanes narrowed to one, as the westbound traffic was routed onto one of the eastbound lanes. The four-lane divided highway became a two-lane road with a concrete barrier in the middle. Traffic backed up, and the bus came to a stop. A few moments later the engine sputtered, then stopped running completely. It had overheated. Car horns started honking. The bus blocked the westbound lane, and nothing could get around it.

"What happened?" Newell asked as he hurried to the front of the bus.

"I don't know," Dave, the driver, said. "We've got plenty of gas. I don't know what is wrong."

"Let me go back and check it out," Newell said. Unfortunately, concrete barriers on both sides made it next to impossible to get out and walk behind the bus. Instead, Newell went to the back of the bus, opened a window, and climbed out onto the barrier. He opened the hood on the back of the bus but didn't know what to do. "I sure wish I knew something about bus mechanics right now," he said. He pushed on a couple of wires and checked the belts and hoses. "Try it now," he yelled.

The bus started right up; apparently the engine had cooled enough. Newell slammed the hood shut, jumped back onto the barrier, and two students grabbed his arms and pulled him back inside. They were again on their way back to Michigan.

Colleen, Carly, and Sandra would not leave Whitney's side. They went with her to her therapy sessions and introduced themselves to Stephanie and the others who had been working with Whitney for the past two weeks. "I guess we're trying to make up for lost time," Colleen told Stephanie. "We've missed so much; we don't want to miss anything else."

Whitney was worn out from all the excitement of the day, so her sessions were shorter than normal. When they took her back to her room to rest, her family was there waiting for her. Sandra sat down next to Whitney and brushed her hair. When she took a nap, Carly snuggled up next to her and slept as well. Colleen sat back and soaked it all in. *I cannot believe this is happening. I cannot believe I have my daughter back.* She caught herself crying throughout the day as she sat and started at Whitney. Her daughter was alive!

She walked over to her bed as Whitney lay sleeping. She had a cast on her leg that, although it was much smaller than the one she had worn in ICU in Fort Wayne, still seemed huge to Colleen. Whitney's left arm was in a sling, and Colleen tilted her head to look at her daughter's left elbow. Then she traced her fingers along the bump where Whitney's collarbone had healed and stroked her blonde hair. "That's quite a look you've got there," she whispered as she touched the place in the front where Whitney's hair had just begun to grow back after being shaved for the spike. Colleen looked closely at the scar where the trach had been in Whitney's throat, and then gazed down at the bandage on her stomach where the feeding tube had been. "You've been through so much, Whit. I'm sorry I wasn't there to go through it with you," she said softly. Looking over her daughter's body, Colleen noticed how thin she had become, especially in her arms and legs. Whitney had always had an athlete's build. Five weeks of lying in a hospital bed had taken much of that away.

One thought intruded on the moment. Standing over her daughter, Colleen couldn't help but wonder, *What if we'd looked at the body? Would I have noticed immediately that a mistake had been made right then, instead of five weeks later? Could we have avoided this whole thing if I'd insisted on seeing her when I got to the hospital that very first morning?* She let out a sigh and tried to push the questions aside, but they kept coming. *What if Carly had looked at the body? Would she have noticed they'd made a mistake? Or Newell? How different would all of this have been if Newell had asked to see Whitney when he flew in from Mississippi?* Her mind raced back to a conversation she'd had with Carly a few weeks earlier, while Carly was back at Taylor finishing up the semester. Carly had wanted to go see Laura at Parkview, but their mutual friend Sara wouldn't let her. She said that no one but immediate family was allowed into Laura's room. Colleen began to wonder why Sara had been so insistent that Carly not go to the hospital, especially since Sara had been there so many times herself, and she wasn't immediate family. *What if Sara had let her go to the hospital? Would Carly have recognized Whitney? I wonder if Sara noticed the mistake, but was afraid to say something.*

A nurse opened the door, snapping Colleen back into the moment. Whitney awoke, rose up in her bed, and held out her arms. Her eyes opened wide. Colleen noticed the sparkle wasn't back yet. "Sorry, sweetheart, it's just me," the nurse said. Whitney lay back down. Throughout the rest of the day and into the night, every time the door opened, she raised herself up, looking for her father. By the early evening she told her mother and sister that she wanted to get ready for her dad's arrival. They gave her a shower, brushed out her hair, and helped her put on makeup.

While Colleen, Carly, and Sandra took care of Whitney, Jim Mathis made the necessary phone calls. Rather than phone everyone in Gaylord who knew the Ceraks, he contacted the local radio station and asked them to announce the news on the air. Newell and Colleen later learned that the town shut down for the afternoon as the news spread. Colleen did call her school to talk to her principal. He immediately called a teacher's meeting to share the good news. The next day the halls and classrooms were abuzz with the news that Mrs. Cerak's daughter was alive.

Mark Vaporis, the friend and coworker who had driven Newell to the airport when he'd received the call that Whitney had been killed, met the bus in Lansing. Newell said good-bye to his students, jumped into Mark's car, and they shot down I-96 toward Grand Rapids. They pulled into the hospital parking lot at ten P.M. Newell looked around and said, "My gosh, why are there so many news trucks here? This is crazy." The hospital had arranged for him to pull around to the ambulance entrance and had sealed it off from the media. He rushed inside, where Colleen, Jim Mathis, and some hospital staff awaited his arrival. "Where is she?" he said.

"Right this way, Mr. Cerak. We've been waiting for you."

Newell dashed down the hall, with Colleen and Jim following behind. Arriving at the room—which now had a sign outside that read Whitney Cerak—he pushed open the door. Whitney rose up and extended her arms. Newell rushed over to her, grabbed his daughter, and wept. Colleen, Carly, and Sandra wrapped their arms around them as well. Newell kissed Whitney on the forehead and told her he loved her. As the five of them embraced, Whitney let out a long sigh of relief, relaxed her shoulders, and said ever so softly to her father, "Let's go home."

18

HOPE IN TRAGEDY

To those who ask, "How could this all have happened?" and would say, "You need to bring a lawsuit," God calls *me* to a response of love and forgiveness. Jesus said, love and pray for those who do you harm. Jesus is our example. He himself suffered unjustly and forgave. He calls us to imitate him. We are here today to celebrate Laura's life.

I invite you to hear the words of Jesus from the book of Matthew. "You are the light of the world. A city on a hill cannot be hidden. Neither do people light a lamp and put it under a bowl. Instead they put it on its stand, and it gives light to everyone in the house. In the same way, let your light shine before men, that they may see your good deeds and praise your Father in heaven."*

It is common practice to say wonderful things about those that have passed away in a moment like this. But today I say in truth, this is how Laura lived her life. Her light shone and continues to shine before people in a way that profoundly affects us all for God's glory. Someone on the blog stated, "I feel as though I have been blind for the first twenty-one years of my life. And your faith and devotion has shown me the light." Our hope today is that all of us will see the one true light, Jesus.

DON VAN RYN'S OPENING REMARKS AT
LAURA'S MEMORIAL SERVICE, JUNE 4, 2006

---

* Matthew 5:14–16.

Don leaned the ladder against the house and climbed up onto the first-level roof. The past couple of days had left him emotionally exhausted. He needed to do something active and installing the air conditioner in a second-floor bedroom fit the bill. He could work with his hands, and no one would bother him while he was up on the roof. Just as he was getting started, he noticed a strange woman walking up their very long, very secluded driveway. He struggled to be civil as he called down from the roof. "May I help you?"

"Mr. Van Ryn?"

"Yes," Don said with an uncertain voice.

She identified herself as a reporter for a local television station. "Mr. Van Ryn, I want to tell you how terribly sorry I am for your loss of your daughter. Would it be possible to ask you a few questions about her passing and the identity switch with the other girl?"

It's already starting, Don thought. "We've issued a statement through Spectrum Health, and that's all we have to say right now," he said, then turned to go back to installing the air conditioner. He didn't want to talk to anyone, especially a reporter.

"Isn't there anything further you would like to say? So many people have followed this story, and they have many, many questions," she said.

"No. Now, if you don't mind, I would kindly request that you leave the property," Don said. The reporter closed her notebook and turned to walk away.

After the woman left, Don climbed down off the roof and walked into the house. "Who was that?" Susie asked.

"A reporter."

"And she walked right up to the house?" Susie said.

"Yep. I doubt if she will be the last. Remember they warned us that the media would be very interested in this story. I guess it's started already. This reporter said people have questions about what happened. I'm sure they do, but I really don't feel any obligation to answer them," Don said.

"If one reporter found us, I'm sure they all will," Susie said.

"What we need are bodyguards," Don joked. Then it struck him, "You know, that's not a bad idea." The next day he gave the job to one of his nephews, a very large nephew. Don posted him at the end of the drive and told him to intercept any and all reporters who tried to come up to the house. "Don't be rude," Don told him, "but let them know we've already made a statement, and leave it at that." By the end of the day the "bodyguard" had turned away nearly a dozen reporters.

Producers from ABC, NBC, CBS, and CNN, along with representatives from shows like *Oprah* and *Dr. Phil* began calling. Magazines and newspapers contacted the family, along with media outlets from other countries. After the second or third call, Don and Susie let the answering machine pick up, then immediately deleted the messages. Many people sent flowers, with some of the biggest bouquets coming from the media. Each had a card that said essentially the same thing: "We are very sorry for your loss. When and if you ever decide to speak to the media, would you please consider granting us an exclusive interview?" At one point during the ensuing week, a helicopter circled around and around their property. The Van Ryns stayed inside and did their best to ignore it. "Some other big news story will break, and they'll all flock to that and forget all about us," Don said during the helicopter episode.

• • •

"That must be the Ceraks," Susie said Friday afternoon as a strange car came up the driveway. The car pulled onto the lawn that had been converted into a parking lot to accommodate all the relatives' cars. Earlier in the day Newell had called, asking if he could come by, and Susie recognized the blonde girl climbing out of the passenger side. "It's them all right," she said.

Newell and Carly walked across the yard as Don walked over to greet them. Colleen had stayed at Spectrum with Whitney. "Thanks for letting us come by," Newell said. "I know how time gets crunched with all the friends and family who want to see you. It means a lot to me that you would take time out for us."

"The feeling's mutual," Don said. "You just don't want to leave her side, do you?"

"No. Not at all." Newell felt guilty answering the question. "I spent most of last night sitting and staring at her as she slept. And I have to say, every time I look at Whitney, I think of you and Laura. I think I probably will for the rest of my life."

Don paused before trying to respond. Susie wiped her eyes, as did Carly. "That's . . . uh . . ." He stopped. Sighed. Then said, "Thank you."

Lisa joined them and they all moved inside to a secluded room to spend some time together. "Carly has told me quite a bit about Laura. They shared a lot of mutual friends at Taylor," Newell said. "I just . . ." He stopped and regained his composure. "I just wanted to come by and tell you how sorry I am for your loss. Laura sounds like she was an incredible girl."

Don and Susie looked at each other and smiled, even as tears welled up in Don's eyes and flowed down Susie's cheeks. "She was," Susie said. "She was one of those unique people who thoroughly enjoyed life, and that rubbed off on whoever she was around. We were talking about this last night as a family, and one of her brother's said Laura exuded joy. That's the best way I know to describe her."

Lisa laughed. "I would second that. Laura loved life. She was always going around here dancing and singing. She would try to get me to dance with her, but she got all the rhythm in the family, not me. I'd try and would end up looking stupid, which would make her laugh and laugh, and I'd laugh with her.

"And we sang together. A lot. I took my guitar into her room both at Parkview and at Spectrum and sang to her. So let me know if Whitney suddenly develops a love for the Dixie Chicks. Laura and I used to sing their songs all the time." They all laughed.

"During the memorial service Brad Larson's dad talked about how much he admired his son and wanted to be like him," Don said. "I feel the same way about Laura. Yes, she was a Christian, but there was more to it than that. She had this incredibly personal faith. God never seemed far away from her and trusting Him completely seemed to come so naturally for her." He looked over at Newell. "I'm sorry if we're boring you. You probably didn't come out here to hear us go on like this."

"No, no. Keep going. I know talking like this about Whitney was really special to us when we thought she was . . . well, before Tuesday."

"You asked for it," Lisa said. "I remember one night Laura and I were sitting out on the porch swing, reading our Bibles together. We were reading somewhere in the gospels, I don't remember where exactly. And we were reading about Jesus and His twelve disciples. And I remember Laura started talking about what it would have been like to hang out with them. The way she talked about it, she made them come alive like real people, not just people in the Bible. That's what God was like for her. She didn't just believe facts about Him. She had this faith that made everything in the Bible come alive."

"Laura also had such a heart for people," Susie said. "I was going through some of the stuff she left behind after she moved off to college, and I came across one of her old journals. I think it was from eighth or ninth grade. And it had all of the usual middle school prayers, like 'Help me on this test.' But as I read through it, I also came across a girl's name I didn't recognize. Laura wrote how this girl seemed lonely and that something had to be bothering her and she wanted to pray for her. I read that and I wondered how many times people are lonely and struggling around me, and I never notice. But Laura noticed. She constantly prayed that God would fill her with his love and kindness."

"I know it sounds like we're making her out to be perfect or something, and I guess that's what people do at a time like this." Don's voice trailed off.

"No, no, no, I understand completely," said Newell. "Everything you're telling me sounds a lot like the girl Carly described to me on the way over. I appreciate your talking about her."

"It isn't easy. The memories . . ."—Susie paused for a moment—"they can be so hard, and yet they give so much joy. I walked into her room yesterday and opened the closet, and there were all these flip-flops. She had so many flip-flops, she could have worn a different pair every day for a couple of months. She even wore them through the winter. As I stood there, looking at her flip-flops, I found myself laughing and crying at the same time." Tears began running down her face.

"I really admired my little sister," Lisa said after a moment, "because she just had this way of being completely at ease in whatever situation she faced. She could be such a girly girl. But then she could get out in the yard and just go at it with our brothers. That was just Laura. I remember times she would stop me when I was on my way out of the house, and she'd say, 'You're not going to wear that, are you?' Then we'd go back upstairs and she would pick out something else, and she was always right in what she picked out." Lisa smiled as she said this.

"I know some people, when they go through a death, they never want to talk about the person who died," Don said. "We're just the opposite. We want to talk about Laura. I think we'll always be this way. We want to keep the memories fresh. People have come by, and they want to cheer us up, and they'll say something about Laura being in heaven, and I know that's true. But the people who help the most are those who tell us their memories of Laura. We really like hearing their stories."

"I know exactly what you are saying," Newell said.

Don continued, "Some of those people who say something about her being in heaven will often say something like 'She's in such a better place, you wouldn't want to make her come back.' I know that's true, but do you want to know my honest gut reaction? I *do* want her back! I want her right back here with us. Is that selfish? I think every parent that has ever lost a child feels the same way."

Newell didn't say anything. He simply looked at Don and nodded as tears welled up in his eyes.

"One of the things that gets us through this is the joy of knowing exactly where she is right now and knowing that we will see her again," Don said.

"Yeah. Yeah. That's right," Newell said.

"Laura was our youngest, which Whitney is for you, right?" Susie said.

"Uh, yeah." Newell cleared his throat.

"Laura kept the house pretty lively. She had these voices that she would do, and it just made me laugh so much," Susie said. "And she loved the color purple. We painted her room purple, and she had this big fleecy purple robe. She loved purple."

"Laura was also an athlete, which I guess Whitney is also?" Don said.

"Yeah, Whitney played three sports in high school, but she doesn't play anything except intramurals at Taylor," Newell said.

"Laura was on the Taylor lacrosse team," Don said. "She played soccer in high school and was recruited by Taylor to play there. She ended up joining the lacrosse team. Her strength, especially her leg strength, was one of the things about Whitney that really reminded us of Laura. Sometimes during the night she'd start thrashing around, and she'd get those legs going, and it would hurt if you got too close. She got me in a scissors hold one night, and I didn't think I would be able to get out," he said with a smile.

Newell smiled as well. "Yeah, Whitney's pretty strong."

"How is she doing?" Susie asked.

Carly spoke up. "She does something new every day. I know a lot of people all over the world are praying for her, thanks to your blog."

"We haven't stopped praying for her," Lisa said. "We just figure all of those prayers we prayed for Laura, the Lord knew who was really lying in that bed."

The five of them spent some time praying together. As they did, Newell knew exactly how to pray for Don and Susie because he'd felt the pain they now experienced. And Don and Susie knew how to pray for the Ceraks. They knew the joy of having a child survive a horrific accident, but also the stress of the uncertainty of that child's prospects for a full recovery. Tears flowed. Both families felt a strong bond with each other.

Two days later, two thousand people attended Laura's memorial service, including many members of the media. It was an oddly public moment for an extremely private family. Church security personnel along with local law enforcement confined the reporters and cameras to one section of the parking lot, far from the family and friends entering and exiting the building. Upon the advice of the media liaison from Spectrum, Don and Susie allowed a single news camera into the church.

As the steady stream of people filed into the large auditorium, the Van Ryns welcomed their extended family—some seventy people in all, including Aryn and his family—into a secluded room backstage. There, away from the prying eyes of media cameras, hugs, tears, memories, and expressions of grief and gratitude

flowed freely. As they all bowed in prayer together in final preparation for the service, Don and Susie sensed God's presence with
them, marveling that the prayers of these seventy were multiplied
many times over through the prayers of thousands just beyond
the door and even around the world. The Lord had been hearing
prayers on their behalf since the first news of the accident, and his
strength would carry them forward.

Susie's heart warmed at hearing the gentle chords of the piano
and violin as they filed into the auditorium. Her sister Bonnie on
piano and Laura's cousin Bekah on violin were completing a stun-
ning prelude, and Susie sensed their love through every note. As
Don took his place behind the podium to open this celebration of
Laura's life, his eyes scanned the faces of the crowd. Everywhere
he looked he recognized faithful people who had visited them in
the hospital, brought food, sent cards, left messages of hope and
encouragement, run errands, driven miles, shared tears and up-
held them in prayer. The body of Christ, his fellow believers, had
cared for his family, and he was ready now to share something as
well. He invited them all to follow Laura's example, to see and
reflect the one true light, Jesus.

Laura's friends, roommates, aunt, and cousin took turns at the
podium, as did her beloved Aryn, her sister and brother, Lisa and
Kenny, and finally the Van Ryns' longtime friend, Mike DeVries,
who had come to the house when Don and Susie broke the news
of Laura's death to their sons. Susie smiled through her tears as
she saw that Laura's friends behind the podium were all wearing
flip-flops, Laura's favorite choice of footwear for any occasion.

She knew Laura would have loved that. Their words washed over Don and Susie. "Laura's laughter and joy . . . funny stories and silly nicknames . . . servant heart, eager helper . . . mentor, example, spiritual companion . . . model of faith, an inspiration . . . gift of putting others at ease . . . compassionate listening ear . . . singing and playing praise and worship songs on her guitar . . . ever-present smile, radiant faith." And in between the words honoring Laura's character and faith-walk, they all sang words of worship to the God Laura loved, the God whose presence she was now enjoying. Such a precious taste of what they would all experience together with Laura in eternity. As the service closed Don and Susie raised their voices as one with the chorus of two thousand, in words of praise that echoed the profound truth, *"I stand, I stand, in awe of you."*

The story, along with thirty-second video clips, was the lead for the news channels across the country that night. A few days later the family had Laura's body removed from the Gaylord cemetery and brought back to Caledonia, where they held a private burial service for her. By the end of the month, just as Don had predicted, another media event grabbed the nation's attention, freeing the Van Ryns from the spotlight.

Throughout the summer of 2006, the entire family closely followed Whitney's progress through the blog that Lisa created and now Carly continued, as well as through personal visits by Don and Lisa. The Van Ryns all decided to continue wearing the bandanna necklaces they'd made and requested that Carly call Lisa as soon as Whitney took her first steps.

Wednesday, June 7, 2006,

This will be our last post from this website, and we want to thank you for your prayers and the support you've shown throughout this entire situation. We continue to lean on the Lord for our strength and will need your prayers throughout these coming days, weeks, and months. We know and trust that God will take care of us—He is always faithful and will remain so, as His Word tells us. Our final encouragement to all is this: Do not hang on to the things of this world too tightly. Life here is but a vapor and there is an eternity ahead. Consider what God calls us to do— "Do not store up for yourselves treasures on earth, where moth and rust destroy, and where thieves break in and steal. But store up for yourselves treasures in heaven, where moth and rust do not destroy, and where thieves do not break in and steal. For where your treasure is, there your heart will be also." *

Let us continue to reach out to those around us who need prayer, love, and encouragement. As you remember the Van Ryn and Cerak families, let us encourage you to look to your neighbors as well. God has called us to love. Within the next 24 hours we will be getting rid of this blog. How the Ceraks choose to update on Whitney's progress is up to them. Thanks again.

Final blog entry posted by the Van Ryn Family

Neither Don nor Susie returned to their jobs until the end of the summer. Both spent as much time as they could at the place that had always been a refuge for them, the Upper Peninsula Bible Camp.

---

* Matthew 6:19-21

There they grieved their daughter while treasuring her memory. Kenny and Mark returned to their jobs and school. Both wanted nothing more than to be free to grieve privately. Lisa, influenced by her experiences working with the therapists at both Parkview and Spectrum, decided to go back to school and become a physical therapist herself. With Laura never far from her mind, she decided to write a letter to Laura just as she had while Laura was away at school.

Dear Laura,

It's hard to believe how long it's been since I've written you! Remember when you were at Taylor and I tried to write or send you something every week?! In fact, I recall that on April 26 [2006] you left me a voicemail telling me about the progress you had made on your senior paper and you said you wanted me to know that my mailings to you had always been a great encouragement.

Well, since it's been so long, let me fill you in. First of all, last spring, our family had this challenging but great opportunity to just drop everything and take care of someone who was hurt in an accident. We cared for her like she was part of our family and it's amazing, maybe even a miracle, how well she's recovered! And at the end of our time with her, it was like one day God just decided to tell the whole world what we'd been doing. In a surprising way, He allowed us and another family to be a witness for Him. It was all really incredible but I'll spare you the details for now. Just know that we wished you could have been there with us and that your life was a great inspiration to us during that time.

Also, last spring, I had the honor of accepting your diploma for you. Well done on graduating from college! But while I was so happy for you, something about it wasn't quite right. It reminded me of grace. It didn't feel right accepting something that someone else had done all the work for. Like how God just asks us if we'll accept His gift.

Another thing I wanted to tell you about is that I've decided to go back to school and work in physical therapy. I know, I know . . . hospitals and things I can't usually stomach. But something's changed. When our family spent time in the hospital I really loved helping out in the therapy sessions. And one thing you've always modeled for me is compassion. Working with people that have been injured or were born with a disease that limits them physically, I'd have a chance to show compassion. So as I put together walking across that graduation stage for you, learning that I may have a gift in working with people that way, and that I want to pick up with your gift of compassion and carry it for you, this seemed like a good way to go. I hope you don't mind, but I use your backpack at school everyday. And I might have taken over some of your clothes as well. Oh, and before I forget, say hi to Brad for me, and tell him I'm looking forward to that ping pong rematch.

I've thought more about dying and about heaven this past year than I ever have. Wondering what it's like to experience moving from this world into eternity. Sometimes when I miss you a lot I try to picture what you might be doing—maybe dancing or singing, or just smiling. And sometimes it just seems to hurt so much that I don't know what to do or what emotion to even have. But a good friend of ours reminded me of something just the other day. She said that death is a result of sin. So this separation that we have from our fellow believers is not how God originally intended it to be. And in that I find two things. First, it tells me that it's OK to be sad or even angry about you not being here any more. And second, I find a tremendous hope because God will make things right. He will restore heaven and earth to it's original state of wholeness and He Himself, will be at the center and we who believe in Him will all be brought back together.

I can only imagine what you're experiencing right now. What it's like to be with Jesus. I wish I could just sit with you, maybe over an Applebee's blondie, and ask you all kinds of questions. But for now, this letter will have to do and I'll just have to wait until I get there. Laura, I miss you terribly and want to be with you but there is still work to be done here. And thinking back to your days on junior staff at UP Bible Camp, it's just like you to squirrel out of here before the work is finished.

Thank you for being a wonderful sister and a friend. I hope to see you soon.

I love you,

Lisa

Letter to Laura from Lisa Van Ryn written some months
after the memorial service

June 2, 2006

I came to your blog via a newspaper's website in Sydney [Australia]. The newspaper did not mention your faith. Yet, coming to this site it is the most overwhelming feature.

I wish I shared your faith. In reading through this blog it is obvious you have something so special there and I wish I did too. I came here saddened over your terrible circumstances and such a dreadful way to lose your daughter and troubled by the hard time you have been through ... and yet here I am, wishing I had what you have. How can that be?

How rich you are. I hope I don't sound callous, I'm just so moved by your blog. I hope you have the comfort, love, and support you need in this hard time.

Anonymous comment left on the blog after
the news broke of the identity switch

19

AFTER THE HURRICANE

Saturday, June 3, 2006

Romans 12:15: "Rejoice with those who rejoice; mourn with those who mourn." We read this verse to Whitney this morning as we spent time in the Word as a family. My dad followed her to physical therapy, where she was put into a wheelchair that allowed her to use her good arm and leg to push herself back to her room!

In speech therapy the therapist has begun to walk her through the events of the past five weeks. Today she just listened and nodded her head as the therapist gave her a very basic rundown. However, her biggest worry of the day is when Hunter is going to arrive. We have called him many times at her request. In the afternoon, we had to transport her to another facility, where she had a CT Scan. My dad, Sandra, and I had to drive in a separate vehicle, so we put in a worship cd we had been listening to for the past 5 weeks to find comfort in. This immediately brought back all the realness of the pain we felt only a few days ago. Our thoughts were focused on the Van Ryns as we put ourselves back in their shoes. We will continue to rejoice with those who rejoice and mourn with those who mourn.

BLOG ENTRY POSTED BY CARLY CERAK

"Mr. and Mrs. Cerak, would you please stay for a couple of minutes?" asked Dr. Martin Waalkes. Newell and Colleen had just watched Whitney endure a neuropsychology test, which her doctors used to gauge her progress. She had not done well.

"We need to discuss your daughter's brain injury and what you might expect over the coming months," he said. "Whitney suffered what is known as a shearing of the brain. That means the brain itself went through a violent twisting on the brain stem. She also suffered a severe blow to the frontal lobe. These injuries damaged cells and also caused connections between neurons to snap. The connections are not permanently severed, but it will take time for them to grow back. A neuron grows at about the same pace as a fingernail. That means the external injuries your daughter has suffered will heal much quicker than the damage inside her brain.

"The best way to picture this is to think of it as a forest that's been struck by a hurricane. When a healthy forest is hit by the storm, it changes. Some of the trees are wiped out completely. Others snap off, although part of the tree survives. Some sustain some damage, but most of the branches remain intact. With time, new trees will grow up to replace the ones that were lost, and the leaves will return to those still standing. However, the forest is always different after the storm. Whitney will also be different after this storm. And, like the forest, she will not recover quickly. I would say that it will take about two years, maybe three, for the forest in her mind to grow back completely."

Newell and Colleen stared at Dr. Waalkes as he spoke. Both had been so elated that Whitney was alive that they had never stopped to consider whether she would ever come back to them completely. Colleen gripped Newell's hands and tears began running down her face. Newell struggled to maintain his composure as he asked, "How full of a recovery do you think she will make?"

Dr. Waalkes paused. "Honestly? I don't know. That's why I said this injury is like a hurricane blowing through a forest. Only time will tell exactly how much the new forest will resemble the old. I can tell you that the treatments and therapies for your daughter are designed to help those injured areas of her brain heal. However, overstimulation can cause greater damage. I know everyone she knows wants to come and see her. That's understandable. But, and this is very important, Whitney's brain needs rest. Think of it this way—when you or I hear a car outside and a television playing along with a dog barking and someone asking a question, we can sort through the noise and focus on the one that is primary. Whitney can't do that. Not yet, at least."

"But she will get better?" Colleen asked.

"Right now, the tests we've given Whitney show she is severely mentally impaired. Will that be the case a week from now or a month from now? There's really no way to know," the doctor said.

As they walked back to Whitney's room, Newell said to Colleen, "I've read Laura's blog every day, and I know it mentioned brain injuries, but I never, ever thought the injuries were this serious."

"From what the Van Ryns told us, she's come so far, so fast. But . . ." Colleen's voice trailed off.

Reality set in as they walked back to Whitney's room. The two of them sat on the foot of her bed and wept. Neither said a word for a very long time. Since the moment Newell arrived from New York, he'd spent much of his time staring at Whitney, marveling that he had her back. Now he began to see her in light of what the doctor had told them. "That look" he'd described at her funeral wasn't there. She showed none of the spark that he'd always taken for granted in Whitney.

"My lips feel dry," she said in a flat, almost monotone voice. Colleen handed her a tube of ChapStick. Newell watched as his daughter moved the tube up to her mouth in a slow, sweeping move of her entire arm, as if it took all of her concentration to do something so simple. The reality of her injuries could not take away the joy of having her back from the dead. However, he wondered what the days ahead might hold.

"Where's Hunter?" Whitney asked.

"Hunter's at home," Newell replied.

"I want to see Hunter," she said.

"We've made arrangements for him to come see you. The hospital said he could come."

"Get Hunter," she said and pointed toward the door.

"Whit, Hunter can't come today," Newell said.

She pointed toward the door and said, "Hunter."

"Whitney, Marty Maxon is going to bring Hunter down later in the week. But it won't be today."

She pointed again. "Hunter."

"Please, please, Whit. Don't ask about Hunter any more. He'll be here in a couple of days."

Once again, she pointed toward the door. "Get Hunter," she said.

Newell let out along, exasperated sigh. "Oh, Whit," he said.

The two of them had this same conversation over and over for the next couple of days. Finally, on Saturday morning, the door of

Whitney's room slowly opened, and Marty poked her head in the room. "Whitney," she said, "I have someone here who wants to see you." She opened the door wider, and the Ceraks' very large, very hairy golden retriever/yellow Lab mix lumbered into the room.

Whitney turned on her side in her bed and let out a shriek of joy. "Hunter!" she cried in what passed as a yell for her. Hunter ran across the room toward her, his paws clicking on the tile floor. She wrapped her right arm around him as best she could. The dog didn't have to jump up onto the bed; he was already on eye level with her. "Missed you, Hunter," Whitney said as she stroked his head. "Love you." After a few minutes, Hunter lay down beside her bed, and Whitney lay back down. She let out a long, satisfied sigh. All of the missing pieces in her life were now back together.

"I can't get over how much she loves that dog," Colleen said. "I think she missed him as much, if not more, than she missed us."

Newell laughed. "Finally," he said, "I won't have to answer her questions about when Hunter is going to get here."

Thursday, June 8, 2006

Whitney had a hard time getting to sleep last night. Finally she found the most comforting place with her mother, Colleen. It was satisfying to wake in the morning to see both Whit and Colleen sleeping peacefully side by side. It sometimes seems the morning comes too quickly, but it is the start of the new day with our daughter, and being able to watch her yawn and stretch makes it seem as though it didn't come quickly enough.

During her occupational therapy time they worked on her elbow extension and contraction. It hurt her, but it is necessary to get that joint to loosen up ... Later that day as she was resting in bed I noticed Whit was placing her right hand on her left arm, giving it a push to extend it and giving a pull to contract it. I asked her what she was doing, to which she replied, "going home sooner." When Whitney, Carly, Colleen, and I were sitting out in the sun, we were commenting on how well Whit had done during the day. Carly said she should be proud, but Whit shook her head no. When she was asked why she wasn't proud, she responded, "I want to do more."

In Christ alone, Whitney's dad

Blog entry

"Matt told me I am in *People* magazine," Whitney said to her parents. Matt and she had been best friends long before they started dating about a year before the accident.

Two weeks had gone by since the family had been reunited, and everyone, including the hospital staff, was amazed at her progress. Whitney's double vision had nearly gone away, her short-term memory had improved significantly, and she was able to speak in longer, more complete sentences. The nurses were eager for her to take another neuropsych test. All were confident she would do much better this time.

"Yeah, Whit. You're on the cover of *People.* There's a story in there about your accident," Newell said.

"Can I see it?" she asked.

Newell and Colleen looked at each other. They'd already told her she had been in an accident, and her therapists had also tried to bring her up to date about all that had transpired over the past nearly two months. Although she knew some of what had happened, her grasp on it remained tenuous. "Okay," Newell said. "I guess that would be all right."

He placed the magazine in her lap and opened to the story about the accident. The first page featured side-by-side photographs of her and Laura. "I don't look anything like her," Whitney said. "Why does this magazine say that I do?" As she turned the page, she saw a photograph of the Taylor van after the accident. "Wow. Was anyone else hurt?" Newell paused. He did not want to answer that question, but he knew he had to. "Yeah, Whit. Five people were killed."

"Who?"

"Laura Van Ryn. Monica Felver. Laurel Erb," Newell said. Tears started running down Whitney's face as Newell continued, "Betsy Smith. And Brad Larson."

A few days earlier, Whitney had talked to Carly about Brad, telling her sister what a great guy he was. When Whitney heard Newell list Brad's name, she said, "Oh no. Not Brad." For several minutes she repeated over and over, "No, not Brad." She set the magazine aside and grew very quiet. "I want to be by myself now," she said as she lay down on her bed. She didn't say anything for a long time as she lay there, softly sobbing. Colleen sat down beside her and started gently rubbing her back until Whitney drifted off to sleep. Throughout the night Newell would awaken to the sound of Whitney crying, and Colleen whispering prayers for her.

A day or two later, Whitney asked to see the magazine again. "Why did they put my picture next to Laura's?" she asked.

Carly was in the room for this conversation. "Whitney," she said, "right after the accident they misidentified you. They thought you were Laura, even though Laura had been killed."

Whitney became very still, trying to process what she'd just been told. The neurons in her brain misfired. Suddenly she grew very upset. "No. That's not right. I did not kill anyone." Tears began pouring down her face, and her body began to shake. "That can't be true. I didn't kill Laura."

"Whitney, Whitney," Carly said, trying to calm her down. "No one thinks you killed Laura. They thought you *were* Laura."

"Everyone will hate me now," Whitney said. "I don't want to go back to school. Everyone will think I am the girl who killed Laura."

"No, no, no, that's not true. No one thinks you killed Laura. Laura died in the accident. People love you, Whit. And they love Laura, too. No one will love you any less because of what happened to Laura," Carly said. Whitney calmed down after she said this.

However, the next evening Whitney became upset again. She looked around the room at her family and her boyfriend, Matt, and said, "None of this is real."

Confused looks shot around the room. "What do you mean, this isn't real?" Colleen asked.

"This hospital bed and these stories about an accident. None of it happened. I'm having a really bad dream, and I wish I would wake up," Whitney said.

Matt walked over and took her hand. "Whitney, could you feel me squeezing your hand if this were a dream?" he said.

"Yeah, because I would be dreaming it! Don't be stupid, Matt. I'm having a dream and all of you are in it. You're in it, and Carly is in it, and Sandra is in it, and my mom and dad are in it. All of you are at the hospital, I'm not really there. I'm in bed in my dorm at school, and I wish I could wake up."

"Whitney, honey, this isn't a dream. You *are* in the hospital. You *were* in an accident. That really happened," Newell said.

"No it didn't. I remember. I worked a banquet at the DC [dining commons] tonight, then I walked back to my room, and then I went to bed. And now I'm having this dream, and I'm really mad at Emily, because she's being a bad roommate and won't wake me up."

Colleen and Newell walked over together to her bed. "Whitney, you need to understand, this isn't a dream."

"Yeah it is. I dreamed you told me that everyone thought I looked like Laura and that I was Laura. I dreamed you told me that you thought I was dead, and that you had a funeral for me. That would never happen. I have to be dreaming."

"Yes, honey, it did happen. Over a thousand people came to your funeral. The line was longer than the line for Disney World," Colleen said.

"Why would people wait so long in line for me? That doesn't make any sense. I want to wake up. I hate this dream. Doesn't Emily know I have to get up? Why won't she wake me up?" Whitney became more and more upset. No matter what anyone said, she would not believe this was anything but a dream.

"Whit, I'm going to call Emily. She's going to tell you that this is real, that you are not dreaming," Newell said. He dialed the number in his cell phone, waited for Emily to answer, and explained the situation to her. Then he handed the phone to Whitney.

"Please, please, please, wake me up, Emily," Whitney said.

"Whitney, you are awake. This is not a dream. If it were a dream, would I be talking to you on the phone right now?" Emily said.

"Yes! If I dreamed it you would!"

"Whitney, you are not asleep. This is not a dream."

"Stop being a bad roommate, Emily. Wake me up. You're going to make me late for class. I'll end up getting a bad grade and my GPA will go down." Whitney began to cry almost uncontrollably. "Just wake me up. I don't want to be in an accident where so many people died. I don't want people to wonder why I survived and their friends didn't. I don't want this to be real."

She began crying to the point of hyperventilating. Colleen stepped out of the room and found a nurse. They finally had to give Whitney a sedative to calm her down and allow her to sleep. When she awoke the next morning, she still wanted this to be a dream, but she understood it was not.

A day or two later, when Matt brought Whitney back to her room from one of her therapy sessions, they found Carly talking to someone Whitney did not recognize. "Hi, what's your name?" she said to the girl.

"Lisa."

"Lisa what?" Whitney asked.

"Lisa Van Ryn."

"Hi, Lisa. It's nice to meet you."

"It's really nice to meet you, Whitney."

"How do you know my sister?"

"I'm a friend of the family," Lisa replied, brushing away a tear. "Carly tells me you're working really hard to get better. That's great."

"I just want to go home. I want to see my friends and my dog," Whitney said.

"What's your dog's name?" Lisa asked.

"Hunter."

"Hunter. I like that name. Your sister told me you go to Taylor."

"Yeah. I can't wait to go back."

"I went to Taylor. I really liked it there."

"Me too."

"Well, it was really great meeting you, Whitney. I hope I see you again."

"Me too."

The next day Whitney again looked through the *People* magazine with her picture on the cover. She paused and started at each of the pictures. As she came to the last page, there was a picture of a girl playing a guitar. "Hey, that's the girl who came to see me yesterday," she said.

Carly looked at the picture. "Yeah, yeah it is. That's Lisa Van Ryn, Laura's sister," she said.

"I should know her, shouldn't I?" Whitney asked.

"That's all right, she remembers you," Carly said with a reassuring smile.

20

FAST FORWARD

Sunday, June 11, 2006

Whitney had a good restful day today. She is still asking about when she is going back to TU to finish her freshman year and when is summer going to start. We have to keep reminding her that she is not in a dream, that all she is experiencing is for real. It is those last several weeks of time that are missing from her memory, and this causes her to feel it is all a dream, and we are part of her dream. As we said last night, this is typical [for people who have suffered brain injuries] but hard to watch her go through. I know you are praying, I sense the Holy Spirit's presence in our lives ever stronger each day. Thank you so much for caring for my family. It truly is a humbling experience—overwhelmingly humbling. God be praised.

She has had a very good day despite the feeling of being in a dream. Today she wanted her eyebrows plucked, and as it happened she kept saying "Ow!" But she did not want Colleen to stop—she thought she was sprouting a unibrow.

Matt came by today, as did Sandra. Both had taken time off from Spring Hill [a Christian camp outside of Grand Rapids where they are working for the summer]. It added to [Whitney's] upbeat day and was a welcome to us all. She is now able to watch movies if she cares to and today she had us all watch with her the movie *Prince of Egypt*. This was followed by some great conversation. Whitney converses with us in complete sentences, making absolutely great sense as she does. In the course of the chat she asked Matt a question, to which he could not remember what the answer was. Whitney's great sense of humor came out when she suggested that it was Matt who should be in this hospital, not her.

In Christ alone, Whit's dad

Sunday, June 18, 2006 [Father's Day]

I was truly impressed with the Father's Day card Whitney personally made. I have to tell you what it said, it was so precious, so please indulge me. Inside the card were these words: "Dad, Happy Father's Day. I'm glad I got to see you again! Good thing I did, huh, Dad? Isn't my card better than Sandra's and Carly's? I think it is, and I am not away this summer. I love you, Dad. Love, Whitney."

Well, I have to tell you this dad's heart swelled and my eyes filled with tears. I thank God for this time that He has given to me to spend with my girls, Whitney, Carly, and Sandra. God has blessed me in ways that are so hard to put into words. In spite of me, He has blessed me, and I am humbled in His presence.

We are praying for a good day tomorrow after such a busy, love-filled time today. I pray you had a good day with your children as well. God bless.

In Christ alone, Whitney's dad

Monday, June 26, 2006,

Whitney has had another good day. After returning here yesterday from her weekend away, she got a good night's sleep. In the morning she returned to her therapies, improving from what she was able to accomplish on Friday. Using the walker, she walked from the little gym down the hallway. I am not sure how far it was, but it was the most she has walked since using the walker. Her arm strength increases through the therapy. She lies in bed and asks to have her leg and arm stretched. She so wants to become independent. She played the basketball game Pig while balancing on her right leg and did an awesome job. In the afternoon there was more work on her leg movement. The files in her brain that were spilled out at the time of the accident keep getting put back in place in her speech therapy. It is such a joy to watch.

Three friends came by today at different times and visited. Whitney's conversation keeps getting better and better. She is engaging and very pleasant to talk with. Her smile keeps radiating her warmth and improvement.

One thing we forgot to tell you about Friday. She had two visitors. Don and Lisa Van Ryn ate lunch with us. It was a sweet reunion, although Whitney does not remember them. She knows that they are the family that took care of her for the first five weeks, and it was good of them to come and share some of that lost time with her. They are such awesome people, and Whitney will always know about what they did for her. We continue to lift them up in prayer for God's strength to support and comfort them. What a tremendous showing of God's love through this wonderful family.

Christ alone, Newell

Monday, July 3, 2006

It is Monday, meaning back to work. Whitney has a full schedule for the next two weeks. [The Ceraks moved her that week from Spectrum to Hope House, another rehabilitation hospital, for the next phase of her therapy.] Her psychologist called it a window of opportunity for her where she is able to have all her rehab under one roof. We are not going to be able to have as much detail on her rehabs as Whitney is wanting a little of her independence back. She was never a momma's girl to begin with, so she is ready for us to stop hovering over her. Part of me is sad because I learned so much watching the therapists work (the teacher side of me), and I loved to see the improvements each session, but the other part is happy because Whitney is gaining her confidence and independence. For the next two weeks she will have at least six hours of therapy each day. On Friday, July 14th, we will have her two-week evaluation, a big meeting with all the therapists and doctors that will tell us where she is at in rehab and how much longer we need to stay. Whitney is working hard each day toward that goal. She is enjoying getting to know her therapists as it is a one-on-one session with each.

Because of the holiday tomorrow, we were able to take Whitney away for the evening. We found a gas grill on the deck, and I actually cooked a real meal. It felt so normal (except missing Sandra) sitting and laughing around the dinner table. Carly got Whitney laughing so hard that I thought I was going to have to perform the Heimlich. After dinner a couple of Taylor friends came, and it again felt so good to hear laughter and the girls talking. Whitney is looking forward to sleeping in tomorrow and of course the fireworks. Hope you all have a great holiday with your families and friends.

Whitney's mom

Wednesday, July 12, 2006

Today Whitney was on her own for most of the day. She did a fine job of ordering her day. She is fast becoming a dynamo when it comes to hopping around. This Tuesday morning she went almost 400 feet, then in the afternoon tacked on another 200 feet plus. So, strength and endurance keep improving.

For her occupational therapy time she was given the tasks of cleaning her bathroom area, doing her laundry, and straightening up her room. She must have completed the jobs in a good fashion, because one of her therapists said to us, "You must have taught her well … most people complain but she didn't … she just went right to work and got it done." Awesome job, Whitney! We thank God she remembered, her room might be clean at home whenever we get back.

In Christ alone, Whitney's family

Friday, July 21, 2006

Whitney looked great again today! That smile, those dimples from before are definitely back. She continues with her daily routine. Today she cleaned the kitchen as well as straightened up her room. I timed her as she scooted down the hallway in the wheelchair; she really moves along now. The strength in her arms is on the increase … yesterday when getting up into the Suburban, she lifted herself up onto the seat.

Her spontaneity is becoming more obvious. By that we are talking about how quickly she responds in conversation. Her facial expression is more and more natural. God continues to strengthen her body and mind. We praise Him for all He is doing.

Tomorrow is a big day! Whitney has a couple of doctor's appointments. One that is most important to her is with her orthopedic surgeon. She finds out if she can weight-bear on that left leg. We appreciate your prayers as Whitney continues on this recovery road.

In Christ alone, Whitney's dad

Thursday, August 3, 2006

Whitney's day today was an awesome day. After going through her regular schedule in the morning, we had a meeting with her entire team of therapists and the neuropsychologist. It is so hard to believe only a little over three months have passed since the accident. The time seems to have gone by slowly. We were reminded at the meeting that Whitney's journey from being diagnosed with a severe brain injury and several broken bones to where she is today is in no way a small miracle. It is a great miracle!! God has been good. The progress in this period of time has been so much more than was expected. Her recreational, speech, physical, and occupational therapists all gave glowing reports of Whit's progress. All were obviously very pleased at how much she improved in the three weeks since her last team meeting. Her neuropsychologist was truly impressed, saying her recovery to this point has been remarkable at the least. There is still a ways to go, but there has been awesome improvement.

The things that are still in need of her concentrated efforts are her neuro endurance and the speed of her processing information. There have been improvements in these areas, for which we are thankful. We continue to pray for complete healing for Whitney.

This was all awesome news ... much better than we expected. Our thoughts before had been guarded optimism that Whitney might attend Taylor in the fall. We knew without a doubt that she would be there in January. But that guarded optimism turned into more with the report. We were given the pros and cons for both situations of school. Either decision would benefit her, but we felt that Taylor would be the place where she would improve the most. Whitney's face lit up brightly as it became apparent what the decision was. She just said that this was the best day of her life and kept on smiling ...

In Christ alone, Whitney's family

August 11, 2006, "Never will I leave you ..."
HERE IS THE MOMENT WE HAVE ALL
BEEN WAITING FOR!!!!!!!!!!!!!
"Never will I leave you; never will I forsake you." So we say with confidence, "The Lord is my helper; I will not be afraid. What can man do to me?" ... Jesus Christ is the same yesterday and today and forever. Hebrews 13:5–6, and verse 8 (NIV)

Hi, everyone reading the blog, this is Whitney!! It feels good to finally be the person who updates you about ... me! These past three months have been life-changing for so many, and everyone has had a different experience, including me.

I can clearly remember the past eighteen years of my life, even up to the banquet before the accident. The next thing I can remember after that is seeing Carly, Sandra, and Mom and crying a lot. I know there is a five-week period that I do not recall. Hearing about it is weird for me, because everyone else has memories about me that I do not. Some people came to visit me at the hospital, and a few of those were the Van Ryns. I know they were with me constantly during the first five weeks, but their visit was all I can remember. They are very nice people, and it was funny to hear how I acted when I first came out of my coma.

When I found out that five other people were killed in the accident, I was really sad. I can vaguely remember part of the ride back to Taylor. We were all laughing and having a good time. I feel so badly for the other families. I don't know why this all happened, but the only good thing about all of this is that the message of God was heard in a powerful way. I know my experience is different from everyone else's, but God has taught me He is FAITHFUL because He is with us every step of the way, even in the hardest times of our lives. And it is clear that He has been with me the last few months. My recovery has been hard work, but I thank God for healing me in every way.

It is strange to find out my family and friends had a funeral for me, but they told me God was faithful even during that time. It is so hard to believe that this story is all over the news and so many people know about me. Even though I don't know many of you who are reading what I am writing about my life, I am so thankful to have had your prayers.

I am just so excited that I am home and going back to Taylor in a few weeks! I can't wait to live my normal life again. So consider this the one and only blog entry from me, concluding this season of my life.

I AM FINALLY HOME, Whitney

21

MOVING AHEAD

August 18, 2006

It is hard to believe that we have been home for over a week. The time has flown as Whitney feels she needs to fit her summer into two weeks. (She is doing a pretty good job of it.) A highlight for all of us was last Sunday, our first Sunday together in our home church since Easter. It was a celebration. We were all nervous and excited to share with our church family how God had met each one of our needs and how He loved us this summer. The church stood and clapped as Whitney and the family walked up to the front. It just happened to be our church's annual picnic, so we had a great afternoon reconnecting and Whitney definitely got her quota of hugs and kisses. It has been great to be home, sleep in our own beds, sit around the table for home-cooked meals and laugh. Hunter (our dog) and Taylor (our cat) are so glad we are home.

Whitney has enjoyed every minute with her friends. It was perfect timing as many of them are starting to head back to college. She loved being able to go to La Senoritas for Wing Night, a special tradition for her and her friends. The weather has been great and she has had a few visits to the lake and some evening bonfires. She has been getting an hour a day of physical therapy to continue gaining back some muscles and endurance. Again, we have been blessed by another great therapist.

As our lives return to normal we continue to pray for those families who are continuing to adjust to the changes.

With love, Whitney's mom

FINAL BLOG ENTRY

Although Whitney had been excited about returning to Taylor, fear crept in once she was back on campus. Immediately prior to her release from Hope Rehabilitation Services, she had taken another neuropsych exam. She had scored far better than on the one she had taken in mid-June, so much better that the therapists called it a miracle, but the results had still left her shaken.

As Whitney walked from her dorm room over to the Odle Arena for the first chapel service of the year, she felt as if everyone was looking at her. She moved closer to her roommate, Emily, and tried to blend in. Every few moments heads would snap around as people recognized her. A group of girls walked past, then quickly turned around. Even though they didn't say anything directly to her, Whitney overheard them say to one another, "Oh my gosh, it's her." She shrank back from the attention. More than anything she wanted to be just another student on campus, like she had been before the accident. She turned to Emily, and said, "I hope I didn't make a mistake. I'm not sure I belong here."

"What are you talking about, Whit? Of course you belong here," Emily said.

"Yeah, maybe," Whitney said. The results of her last neuropsych exam kept ringing in her head. *Eighth-grade level. I scored at an eighth-grade level . . . and I'm back at college? I'm basically a middle schooler trying to go to college. I can't believe I thought this would work.*

Amy and Anne met them at the door. "Let's sit over here," Amy said as she led the way. The four of them walked into the middle section of the rows of folding chairs on the basketball floor and sat down. Crowds of students filled in around them. Again, heads turned as people recognized Whitney. One or two said, "Hey, Whitney, how are you doing? It's good to have you back." She smiled and said "fine" and "thank you," while inside she thought, *I can't wait for all this attention to go away.* One of Taylor's student worship bands kicked off the service. Whitney and her friends stood and sang along with everyone else in the gym. Heads stopped turning as the students focused on the worship songs instead of Whitney. She and her friends clapped and sang and lost themselves in the music. *This is what I was waiting for.*

After the music ended, Taylor's president stood to address the crowd. He welcomed the students back to school and talked about his high expectations for the semester. Then came the moment Whitney had dreaded. "We have a miracle in the room with us today." *Oh no. Please don't say it, please don't say it.* "As you remember, the Taylor community was dealt a horrific blow last semester. We lost five wonderful, courageous individuals." *No, no, no, no, please only talk about those five.* "But Whitney Cerak survived the accident, and even though she was very badly injured, she is back with us right now, today." The entire gym erupted in applause. Whitney sunk down into her seat and wanted to disappear.

"It's okay, Whit," Emily said, "after today, things will get back to normal, you'll see."

"I hope so," Whitney said.

The first few days back in class proved to be the most awkward for everyone. Both faculty and students alike wanted to let Whitney know how excited they were about her recovery, but they didn't want to overstep their bounds. Because of how good she looked on the outside, most people assumed she'd also made a full recovery from her brain injury. That was not the case. Newell and Colleen had agreed to allow her to go back to school because her doctors assured them that the stimulation would help the trees blown down by the hurricane grow back faster and stronger. Whitney took a downsized course load, only six credit hours including a golf class, and went to Fort Wayne three times a week for additional therapy. However, the unique schedule made her feel more out of place. Even though the university provided a special tutor to work with her, she struggled to keep up.

Three weeks into the fall semester, Newell saw Whitney's name on the caller ID on his cell phone. "Hey, Whit, it's good to hear your voice," he said. This wasn't a figure of speech. Since the day Colleen had called to tell him that Whitney was alive, Newell treasured the sound of his daughter's voice.

"Dad," she said with a tone that immediately told him something was wrong, "I want to come home."

"What's wrong?"

"I hate it here. I don't belong here. I don't want to be here." Whitney began sobbing into the phone. "I'm not me anymore, Dad, and I hate that. I know I've changed, and I know everyone around me wonders what happened to the old Whitney. I'm not funny any more. I don't want to be around people. I'm not me."

Newell didn't know what to say. If he acted on his feelings, he would have already jumped in his car and taken off for Taylor. He missed her terribly. The distance between Gaylord and Upland had never seemed greater. "Whit, honey, try to stick it out this one semester, and then we'll talk about it."

"Why would God do this to me? Why would He let me be in that accident and then come back to school? I'm a middle schooler, Dad. I'm just on an eighth-grade level. I don't know how I expected this to work," she said.

"Have you talked to Carly about this?"

"Yeah, we've talked about it a ton."

"And what did she say about it?"

"Not much. She mainly just listened. And she said what you said. She said to stick it out to the end of the semester."

"Can you?" Newell asked.

"I don't know. I can try," Whitney said.

Over the next two months, Newell received variations on this same phone call several times. Although all the therapists said she was coping quite well with all she'd gone through, deep down Whitney felt depressed. She had worked so hard to get back to school, but now that she was there, she could not help but feel she didn't belong. Every day felt like an uphill climb, academically, socially, and emotionally, and her father was one of the few people Whitney could tell about it.

A few days before Whitney and Carly were due to drive home for the Thanksgiving holiday, the home phone rang. "I'll get it," Newell said as he grabbed the handset off a table.

"Dad." It was Whitney, but the tone of her voice was completely different.

"Hey, Whit, how are you?" he said.

"I took another neuropsych test, and they just gave me the results."

"Yes. And?"

"They told me I'm now on a college sophomore level!" She sounded as if she'd just won the lottery.

Tears began streaming down Newell's face.

Colleen, fearing bad news, asked, "What's going on?" Newell couldn't speak. He handed her the phone and sat down and wept. "Whitney, it's Mom. Is everything okay?"

"Yeah, Mom, everything is great. They just gave me the results of my last neuropsych test. I'm at a college sophomore level, right where I'm supposed to be. Can you believe it?"

"Yeah, Whit, yeah I can. I never doubted you for a minute," Colleen said. They talked for a few more minutes. Just the sound of her daughter's voice let Colleen know that Whitney would not drop out of school at the end of the semester.

After she hung up the phone, Colleen and Newell held each other and wept uncontrollably. Their daughter had turned another corner, experienced another miracle.

I do not know what to say!
God, you are my refuge — please protect me.
You are my strength — I am entirely weak.
You will give me peace and comfort — please see me through
   the days ahead.

The final entry in the prayer journal Susie started
on April 26, 2006. The journal was to be a gift to Laura
after she returned home.

Susie sat down in the rocking chair on the enclosed porch of the family cabin and stared off toward the dining hall through her open door. Lisa and Julie, her friend with whom she was on the phone the night of the accident, were still asleep in the back bedroom. A few campers ran by, yelling at one another with that playful children-at-camp yell. Others were still in their cabins on the other side of the camp, away from the staff residences. Even though the calendar said July, the early morning air had a cool bite to it. Susie hardly noticed. She sat in the rocker and stared. Her Bible lay in her lap, open to the book of Proverbs. Although she'd found such comfort and strength there since the night of the accident, she didn't feel like reading it this morning. She didn't feel like doing anything. Getting out of bed had been enough of an accomplishment.

If she'd had her way, she would have pulled the blankets up tight over her head and not moved. But she knew she had to get up. She had to force her legs over the side of the bed, and she had to force her body to follow their lead, all because she knew she had to. Once her body was up, she'd managed to get dressed and brush her hair and do all the other things she needed to do to face the day. But she'd made it only as far as the chair on the porch.

As she stared out the window, watching more campers trickle out of their cabins and over toward the dining hall of the camp, she thought how cruel it was that life kept dashing by. She looked down at her Bible, but the letters on the page all ran together into one long, incomprehensible word. She looked harder and could make out the words to one verse that seemed to jump off the page, "Each heart knows its own bitterness, and no one else can share its joy." * *Bitterness and joy mixed together, that's what I feel. Oh, God, how?*

---

* Proverbs 14:10

The high-pitched sound of little girls laughing pulled her attention off the page in front of her and back outside. *Don't they know?* Susie thought. *Don't they know that the world has stopped?* She was filled with sadness that life in a fallen world could dish out such cruelty and not miss a beat.

Oh, God, why? she prayed. *Why does life keep going on when I want it to stop? Why does it keep going forward when I can't move?* She sobbed and stared for a few minutes more before realizing that she had to get up. Sitting in a chair in the quiet seclusion of her cabin was better than lying in bed with the covers over head, but not much. As she tried to muster the strength to stand, she turned her attention to the photograph hanging on the wall just to the side of the door, taken by Don the previous summer. Kenny, Mark, and Lisa had all been working, and Laura had an internship in the Detroit area. But one week last summer, they had all made it up to camp, and Don had taken the picture of them now hanging on the wall of the Chipmunk Inn. The memory of that day, like all the memories of Laura that came flashing back in this place, was bittersweet. Susie chose to focus on the sweet. It gave her the strength to stand up and walk out the open door.

As she walked the hundred or so yards from her cabin to the dining hall, a camper ran by and said, "Good morning." Susie smiled and waved as the girl ran on past. The sound of laughter and the clanking of pots and pans grew louder as she got closer to the dining hall. She climbed up the porch steps and slipped into the kitchen through the back door. It was Pancake Day. On the weeks during the summer when Don was at camp, he always insisted on cooking the pancakes. Susie could picture him standing next to the griddle, dressed like the crazy Irish pancake chef, wearing the rugby jersey Mark had purchased for him while studying abroad in Ireland for a semester.

"Good morning, Aunt Suz," said one of the many students who worked in the kitchen through the summer. At the sound of her name, several others turned. Although Susie had been the chief cook every summer since Don's mom had handed her the reins twenty years earlier, she hadn't spent a lot of time in the kitchen this year at camp.

"Good morning," Susie said, "everything going okay in here today?"

"Just great. Couldn't be better, even though it's Pancake Day. And you know what that means."

"It's a crazy day," Susie said, finishing the girl's sentence. "But it will be crazier next week during boys' camp. The girls don't eat quite as much as the boys, but they come pretty close." The girl laughed. Susie walked on through the kitchen, sharing smiles and greetings with all of the staff, then circled around to the back door. "It looks like everything is under control. Keep up the good work," she said as she reached for the handle.

Her sister-in-law Ruthann, was in the kitchen office just to the right of the door. The two shared a look and Ruthann knew immediately what kind of day Susie was having. Her own son Matt had died five years earlier in a car accident not far from camp.

Once outside, Susie started to go back to her cabin, but thought better of it. The wind whistled through the pine trees and a chipmunk shot from one hole to another just to the side of the dining hall porch. Susie took a deep breath. *Just keep moving,* she said to herself, *just keep moving.* She thought back to the morning in the ICU in Fort Wayne when she walked into the room and saw Laura—no—Whitney, sitting in a chair. The sight had horrified her. Susie remembered thinking how cruel the nurses were for forcing her daughter—no—this badly injured girl, to move when she obviously needed to do nothing but lie still and heal. But they weren't being cruel. Whitney needed to get up and move for the healing process to begin. Now Susie was the one who had to get up and move or her healing process would never begin. This seemed just as cruel, but she knew it was just as necessary.

Just keep moving, she said to herself as she walked from the dining hall across the campground. This camp was a place of refuge and rest for her and the rest of the family. And that's what they needed. Susie knew she had to keep moving, but that didn't mean rushing back to life the way it had been before the accident. She'd taken an extended leave from her job as a hairdresser. The other women she worked with were taking care of her clients while she was away, just as they had since the end of April. The staff had even put together a money tree for her to help cover the expenses her family incurred through the spring and summer. Work could wait. Susie knew she needed to be here, not just for a weekend or a week or a month, but for the summer.

As she crossed the campground, she heard the slam of a screen door, then another. Campers poured out of the cabins and rushed toward the dining hall for breakfast. She could hear Laura laughing, could see her running with the rest of the girls. Although the Van Ryns owned a cabin on one end of the campground, ever since she first attended girls' camp Laura had stayed with the rest of the campers in the long dormlike cabins.

Moving farther away from the dining hall, Susie walked up to the campfire pit. At least one night each camp session, the counselors built a large fire and all the campers gathered around. Susie could picture Laura and Lisa sitting next to the fire pit, playing their guitars, leading the rest of the camp in worship. Lisa had taught Laura how to play, and the two loved playing together. In between the shouts from the campers Susie could almost hear the sound of her daughters singing. She smiled as tears began running down her cheeks.

Then she sat down on a bench just off the sandy shore of the lake. Susie couldn't help but think about the day sixteen years earlier, on that very same beach, when Laura had asked one of the camp counselors to pray with her. She had been thinking about God and Jesus and all the truths from the Bible she'd heard from the time she was born. That day, as a six-year-old child, Laura sat with the counselor on the sandy beach and prayed a simple prayer, asking Jesus to be her Savior. Not long afterward she wrote her first song. Lisa had read the lyrics during Laura's memorial service. They had never sounded sweeter.

> *Little girl sitting on the beach*
> *She asked her friend what lessons she could teach*
> *Could it be that Jesus died for you?*
> *Could it be that Jesus died for me?*
> *Could it be He died to save our sins?*
> *Could it be He is coming again?*

Please God help, help me to understand
Please help me, Lord
I want to pray that prayer
I want to go out and share
With the people that do not care
About you, Lord.

Susie smiled at the innocence of the words. *Your faith was always so strong, even from the start. All you ever wanted to do was share God's love with others.* "Oh, Laurie, you seem so close and yet so far away."

The sun rose higher in the sky and warmed Susie as she sat there, next to the lake, "little girl sitting on the beach" ringing in her ears. *Oh, God, help me*, she prayed. *I am so weak . . . but you are my strength.*

EPILOGUE
From Whitney

Most of what you just read was as new to me when I read it as it was to you. Several times while I was reading, I said, "Wow, did that really happen?" and "Did I really do that?" I don't remember anything between getting in the Taylor van in the parking lot of some mom-and-pop pizza place in Fort Wayne on the night of the accident, and waking up in Grand Rapids one day in June with my mom and sister and Sandra in the room with me. When I saw them I remember crying, but I don't remember why. And I remember Stephanie, the speech therapist, saying, "Yep, that's how you know it's real, because she's so emotional about it." I'm not sure what that means, since I wasn't really in a good state of mind to figure it out, but it's one of the first things I remember after the accident. Everything else is a blank.

People tried to tell me everything that happened to me after the accident, but I never knew all the things in this book, especially all the things the Van Ryns went through. Lisa apologized to me not long ago for not realizing I wasn't Laura sooner. I told her to stop it and never say that to me again. The Van Ryns have nothing to apologize for! I love them, and so appreciate all they did for me. They are amazing. I think most people would be mad about what happened, but they aren't. They have never acted like *why did you survive and not Laura?* They've done the exact opposite.

When our families got together on the one-year anniversary of the accident, my mom told them that she struggled talking with them because our family had the happy ending. Don looked right at me and said, "So did we. We just haven't seen all of it yet." That meant so much to me. Their entire family has made it very clear to me that my recovery is an answer to all the prayers they prayed going back to the night of the accident. Just the fact that they could feel that way toward me is amazing.

As you read in the last chapter, I struggled after the doctors cleared me to go back to my real life. One of the things I struggled with was the fact that I was the only student to survive the accident instead of one of the others. I didn't really know Laura or Laurel. Brad and I weren't good friends, but I knew him well enough to know that he was amazing. Betsy I loved. I had a class with her, and she made me feel so special, even though I was just a freshman. I would be walking across the campus and I would hear someone yell, "Hey, Whitney," and it would be Betsy, smiling and waving at me. She had such a heart for people. I can't believe she's gone now. Even though I didn't know the others who died in the accident well at the time, the more I learn about them, the more I realize they were incredible people. At times last year I would look at myself and compare myself to them. They all loved God so much, and all of them would have done wonderful things for Him. Why did God keep me here and not them? It didn't make any sense to me.

My dad and I talked a lot about this in our phone calls. One night he finally said, "Whitney, why not you? It could have been anyone who survived. It all just came down to who was sitting where in the van. You don't have to feel guilty for surviving." I thought a lot about what he said, and finally it started to make sense to me.

At the one-year memorial, Don Van Ryn said that any one of the people in that van would have gladly given his or her life for Christ. And I believe that is really what they did. Since the accident, and since the mix-up with Laura and me, so many people have heard and seen God's love that wouldn't have heard it any other way. People wrote into the blog, telling how they had become Christians because of this story. Other people became Christians at my funeral and at Laura's. Don said that's what all the people in the van would have wanted, no matter what the cost. Hearing him say that helps me realize God can work through anything, good or bad. I still wonder, though, if only one student was going to survive, why it was me and not Betsy or Brad or Laurel or Laura. I still don't get that. Maybe I'm not supposed to. Even if I can't figure it out, I know that God has a purpose for it, even if I never completely understand what it may be.

Knowing God has a purpose, however, didn't exactly make life easier. After I went back to school, people came up to me all the time and said things like, "God isn't finished with you. He's got something great in store for you." I never knew what to say in return. I knew they all meant well, but I don't think any of them realized how hard it was to be on the other end of that statement. You read in the book that my dad and I watch *Saving Private Ryan* on Memorial Day every year. At the end of that movie, Tom

Hanks's character says to Private Ryan with his dying breath something like, "Earn this." It's like he's telling Private Ryan to do something so special with his life that it will make the other soldiers' deaths worth it. That's kind of how I felt when people told me how God must have some great purpose in mind for me. I started to think that if I didn't do something amazing with my life, then I was letting God and everyone in the accident down.

One day I was having coffee with a friend named Brad, and I told him a little about how I'd been feeling. In response, he read me a story from the Old Testament book of 1 Kings. In the story, a prophet named Elijah goes out in the desert to talk to God. He's waiting for God when he hears this giant windstorm that is so strong it tears the rocks apart. But God isn't in the windstorm. Then there's an earthquake, but God isn't in the earthquake. Then there's a fire, but God isn't in the fire. Finally, he hears a gentle whisper, and he realizes that it's God. Another friend had read the same story to me during my freshman year, so I knew God was telling me something through it.

I realized that instead of thinking that my life has to be some big windstorm or earthquake for God, perhaps I only have to let Him whisper gently through my life. That story made me realize I don't have to accomplish some giant thing for God. If I'm just a camp counselor who makes the difference in the life of one person, or if I'm just a mom who loves her children and tells them about Jesus, that's enough. It took a little while, but I finally figured out that God's purpose is for me to let Him do whatever He wants in my life, big or small. Being a part of writing this book may be the last "big" thing I ever do, and I'm fine with that.

The accident and everything that followed has changed me. I'm the only person I know who's listened to her own funeral. That was pretty weird. I did that once, and once was more than enough. I'm glad they didn't make a DVD of the service. I don't think I could watch it.

I also find it very strange how people I've never met feel a connection with me. Once a complete stranger came up to me with tears in her eyes. She started telling me how her daughter had followed my story every day on the blog, and she wanted to take my picture for her little girl. That was weird.

It was also weird to see my picture in *The National Enquirer* and *People* magazine, which both called Laura's and my story one of the biggest news stories of 2006. That strikes me as odd. A lot of what was written in different magazines was wrong, and I think it gave me a different perspective on people and the media that I never had before.

I really am a different person than I was before. I used to be a lot more outgoing and I joked about everything, but my brain injury affected my personality. Now I keep a lot more to myself. Before the accident, I could whip out jokes and make quick, funny comments in any situation. Right after I went back to Taylor, my brain still hadn't healed enough for me to do that. I would be with a group of people and someone would say something funny, and I would start turning it over in my head, trying to think of something to add to it. By the time I could think of something, the moment would have passed. I'm much better now, but I'm still more reserved than I used to be.

Coming to grips with being a different person was probably

the hardest thing I struggled with. I knew my cognitive abilities would improve, and they have. The doctors told me that those areas of the brain that affect my schoolwork are some of the last to heal after an injury like mine. But they *are* healing. I can see that. Finishing college would be a little easier if they would heal faster, but I'm just happy I was able to go back to school. My personality, however, is still different than it was before the accident, and it's not going to go back. That has been hard for me, and it was one of the things that made me want to leave school. I know people wondered what had happened to the old Whitney, and I wondered that myself.

Because I am different, I've had to trust God in a way I never had before. When I first went to Taylor as a freshman, I prayed that God would give me a real passion for Him. I grew up in a pastor's home, and going to church and talking about Jesus were pretty much who we were. But I didn't have that burning desire to know God more; I didn't love Him with all my heart, soul, mind, and strength. The accident changed that. When I found I couldn't open up to the people around me and be myself, I opened up to God. As a result, He answered my prayers and gave me a desire for Him that I never had before.

That doesn't mean this has been easy for me. The one person who kept me at school that first year back was my sister Carly. We set up a special sister time where we ate lunch together, once a week, just the two of us. One day, right before spring break 2007, I was feeling sorry for myself. I told Carly I really missed the old Whitney. And Carly, she looked across the table at me and said, "Yeah, I miss the old Whitney too. But I love the new Whitney."

I cannot tell you how much that meant to me. The more I thought about what she said, the more I realized I am fine with who I am now. Yes, I'm different. I'm not the person I was before the accident, but that's okay. I don't want to go back and try to get back someone that's gone forever. Carly set me free to just be me, the new me, the me that God made me to be, wherever that may lead.

IN HONOR OF THOSE LOST

All of the empathy, support, encouragement and healing in the world can never erase the profound loss of five lives. As you have seen in our story, no two families, no two people, respond to loss in the same way. The journey of grief and healing is ultimately a profoundly private journey and we have done our best to dare not speak for or violate the privacy of the other families who lost loved ones. We invited the other families to include a tribute to the loved ones they lost. A few, not all, of those families chose to accept that invitation and we have deep respect and understanding for those who did not and those who did. It is our privilege, therefore to include the following tributes from some of the other families.

—The Van Ryn and Cerak families

Laurel Erb

Some gifts are without measure. For those who loved Laurel, she was both the gift and the giver. Not only did God bless her with an insatiable and highly contagious joy in the beauty of his creation, but she was an amazing example of his artistry as well.

Laurel's life reflected grace, beauty, creativity, hospitality, laughter, and compassion. Her grace and compassion were demonstrated as a five-year-old on hands and knees when she provided her back as a "step-up" for her brother to reach the drinking fountain, and later, as a young woman, she assisted in the monthly financial support of a young girl living in Thailand. Laurel joyfully shared of her time and talents.

God blessed Laurel with immense creativity. She recognized and claimed his promises in the glory of nature. She saw beauty in things that most of us view only as mundane. Her imagination soared when it came to appreciating the largest or smallest facets of God's creation: a sunset, ice formations, the underside of a leaf.

God blessed Laurel with a sense of adventure and an enthusiasm for exploring His creation. He instilled in her a desire to challenge both herself and others, not only in everyday matters, but in ways that encouraged spiritual and emotional growth as she pushed herself to face and conquer situations that intimidated her.

More than anything. God immeasurably blessed us in allowing us to be a part of her life. We wait impatiently to see her again.

—The family of Laurel Erb

Monica Felver

It is hard to sum up the person who we call MOM. She was the hardest worker, loyal friend, honest, loving, truest person we have ever met. To just call her Mom is taking a lot away from her because she was so much more. She was the one we would turn to for everything and anything, our rock. Spending time with her was the best time ever. She would cook a wonderful meal for us and want us to eat several helpings, but we never could. She loved to sit at the table to eat as a family. Her family meant everything to her.

Mom's favorite time of year was spring. She would love to be outside cleaning, gardening, pulling weeds, but nothing said spring like hunting for mushrooms. She loved to go out and see who could find the most. This is something she could do for hours. She could spot a mushroom while we could look in the same spot and still not see it.

Mom loved her animals probably as much as she loved us kids. She had goats, horses, cats, dogs, wild turkeys, chickens, and a lot of fish in the pond. She had several animals that were old and every day she would say how blessed she was to still have them with her.

We may have lost a mom, wife, grandmother, aunt, sister and friend for now, but look forward to her beautiful welcome in heaven.

—The family of Monica Felver

Brad Larson

At the time of his death, Bradley Jesse ("Beej") Larson was on schedule to graduate magna cum laude in May 2006 from Taylor University. Born into the loving family of Dr. David and Sherry Larson, Brad would have joined siblings Jeffrey D. (2002) and Dawn E. (2004) as Taylor alumni. Although Brad majored in history, he trained himself well in a broad range of disciplines — especially in how they relate to the Christian faith — in preparation for graduate studies in law. He was admitted to matriculate at the University of Wisconsin School of Law in the fall of 2006.

Brad was sweet, thoughtful, smart, and athletic. He was fun-loving and had a keen sense of humor. He loved NBA basketball and could discuss basketball trivia for hours. He is remembered by those who knew him as quiet and serious, gifted and good, a role model for his peers. Brad was mature beyond his years and tremendously disciplined. His friends often remarked how much they admired his relentless self-denial and how he held others accountable without any airs of condescension or judgment. He is dearly missed.

> *A shoot will come up from the stump of Jesse;*
> *From his roots a Branch will bear fruit.*

The Spirit of the Lord will rest upon him—
The Spirit of wisdom and of understanding,
The Spirit of counsel and of power,
The Spirit of knowledge and of the fear of the Lord—
And he will delight in the fear of the Lord.
—Isaiah 11:1–3a (NIV)

—David and Sherry Larson

ACKNOWLEDGMENTS

From the Van Ryns

Above all else we acknowledge our Savior, the Lord Jesus Christ, who is at work in our lives constantly to make us more like Himself.

The Van Ryn family would like to acknowledge our immediate family, without whom we would be lost. Their ongoing expressions of love in so many ways are deeply appreciated and will never be forgotten.

We wish to acknowledge our close friends who also came alongside and cared for us through this tragedy, friends from our church and from the Upper Peninsula Bible Camp family. They made many sacrifices and supported us in so many tangible ways. We are grateful for the many friends and family who traveled long distances to be in Fort Wayne with us.

We will never, never forget the love that Aryn Linenger had for Laura, and we honor the entire Linenger family for the love and friendship they showed to us.

We have a special place in our hearts for Laura's roommates

and friends at Taylor University. We cherish our ongoing relationships with her very close friends.

We're thankful to Lindsay Dobson Veitch, who was also one of Laura's dearest friends.

Heartfelt thanks to the worldwide Taylor community and the expressions of love that you have shown us. We thank all who have given to Laura's memorial funds both at Taylor and at Upper Peninsula Bible Camp.

We are thankful for those new friends we got to know in Fort Wayne at the hospital and in the community. What great care we received there!

We're thankful for the wonderful care Whitney received from the fine staff at Spectrum Continuing Care Center in Grand Rapids. We enjoyed getting to know all of you and appreciate your work on our behalf.

There are no words to describe our gratitude to those around the country, and indeed the world, who made gracious comments on our blog. Many of you sent cards to us with prayers and kind thoughts. All of these were a blessing and encouragement to our family.

We want to say thanks to the Cerak family for their gracious love and continuing friendship.

Lastly, we are privileged to have worked alongside a wonderful team of talented people in the writing of this book. Thanks to Wes, Mark, Cindy, and Liz; it has been a blessing!

From the Ceraks

It is hard to know where to begin to thank all those who have played a part in this time in our lives. We hesitate because we do not want to leave anyone out, and yet as we say thanks, please know that these acknowledgments scratch only the surface of people who should be recognized. Those who have played a part, have our heartfelt gratitude.

We want to thank all of you who prayed and who continue to pray for everyone involved. It has been those prayers and faith in God that have sustained, comforted, and brought healing in a miraculous way.

To our immediate families, who have lifted us with comforting and encouraging words and love for us, we thank you with all our hearts.

To the people of Gaylord, Michigan, a very fine community in which to live. Your respect and protection of our family is more than we deserve. For all your support we humbly thank you.

To the folks at the Gaylord Evangelical Free Church, to those senior-high counselors who stepped in for us, to the staff who gave us freedom to spend all that time away, to Deb Harlukowicz who runs interference for us, to Jim Mathis who has been with us from the beginning, you all have a very special place in our hearts.

Thanks to the Gaylord Intermediate School staff and student body for your support and comfort. You all were a blessing to us in our time of need.

While we were missing from Gaylord, so many watched over and took care of our home and our dog, Hunter. To the Steffes,

Volants, Coburns, Maxons, Bowmans, and all those in our neighborhood, please accept our thanks.

To the caregivers at Spectrum Health Continuing Care, Hope Network Rehabilitation Services, and Fort Wayne Rehabilitation: your care of Whitney was far beyond ordinary. A deep heartfelt thanks to you as well.

A special thanks to all those rescue and emergency workers who continue to serve all our communities so well. Your efforts will be forever remembered.

To Taylor University for its gracious way of caring for Whitney. And to Scott Gaier, for your personal involvement, which helped her to succeed in college.

Thank you to Charlie Ward and his dad, Don, for helping us when we had no idea which way to go to make certain that Whitney would be cared for.

A very special thank you to all those who sacrificed to drive Whit to therapy in Fort Wayne: Tim and Kathy Hermann, Marty Songer, Jeanette Hoeksema, Linda Sebastian, and college friends.

To Whitney's roommates, Emily, Amy, Anne and friends at Taylor University for standing by and loving her. You will never know how much we feel indebted to you.

To Matt Wheeler, who was there through it all. You are such a good friend, not only to Whitney, but to the entire family. You treated Whitney perfectly though all of this. We can never say thank you enough.

To Sara VanWinkle, Christine Livingstone, and Brittany Long. You are the unspoken heroes. You stayed by Whitney's side those first weeks and your continued love, strength, and wisdom have been vital to Carly.

To Rick and Shelly Froysland for all you have done; it was a great Father's Day and Fourth of July. There could be no better friends. We love you and thank you.

To the Van Ryns for your care and love of Whitney and for your sweet friendship. We are of kindred spirit, and we thank God for you. You are in our prayers every day.

To those who have worked with us on this book to bring it to reality: Wes Yoder, Mark Tabb, and Cindy Lambert. We have great new friends in you. Thank you.

And lastly, but most important, thanks to our Lord and Savior Jesus Christ. Without God's comfort and strength, we would have failed in our humanness. Through His grace we hope, not as the world hopes, but knowing without doubt that those who have accepted His gift will have an awesome reunion in His presence.

From Mark Tabb

Thank you to Cindy Lambert for entrusting this project to me and to Wes Yoder for working so hard to make it happen. Thank you as well to Liz Heaney, the best editor any writer could ever ask for.

I would also like to thank my home church, Brandywine Community Church, for praying this book through to completion. This project would never have come together without you.

The Van Ryn family—Don, Susie, Lisa, Kenny, and Mark—of Grand Rapids, Michigan shares an avid interest in outdoor recreation. Don and Susie, married for thirty years, are leaving their chosen professions to dedicate themselves full time to an outdoor camping experience for youth in Michigan's Upper Peninsula.

Lisa is pursuing a career in physical therapy, and Kenny lives and works in Southern California. Mark is recently married and resides in the Detroit area.

Despite the sorrow surrounding the passing of their daughter Laura, the family continues to be involved in the work of their local church and community.

The Cerak family—Newell, Colleen, Carly, Whitney and Sandra Sepulveda—lives in northern Michigan, where Newell is a youth pastor and Colleen is a PE teacher and coach.

Carly graduated from Taylor University and has lived in Africa for the last six months starting a new ministry to street kids.

Sandra took a year from Grand Valley State University and joined with Invisible Children to bring awareness of the plight of children in Uganda. She is currently back at GVSU finishing her nursing degree.

Whitney is now a junior at Taylor University majoring in psychology. She is confident in God's healing and the revelation of the Holy Spirit in her life.

Mark Tabb has authored or coauthored twenty books, including the 2004 Gold Medallion finalist *Out of the Whirlwind*. He collaborated with Stephen Baldwin on the New York Times bestseller *The Unusual Suspect*. He lives in Indiana.